Gemma Ray

CW00802154

Self Discipline: A How-To Guide to Stop Procrastination and Achieve Your Goals in 10 Steps

Including 10 day bonus online coaching course to master self discipline and build daily goal-crushing habits

ISBN 9781790329618

www.mindandbodyworld.com

Contents

Self Discipline

With the most grateful heart, I dedicate this book to:

Ben Jones

The greatest accountability buddy the world has ever known, who became my closest ally from the other side of the globe.

Thank you for your unrivalled patience and support. I could not have done this without you.

It is directly thanks to you that I have achieved a childhood dream and my biggest ever goal to date. I write these words of thanks with the biggest smile and happy tears in my eyes.

"We will win"

Self Discipline

Prologue

"One of the most important keys to success is having the discipline to do what you know you should do, even when you don't feel like doing it." **- Unknown**

A note to the reader.

Hi, I'm Gemma Ray, and it has always been a lifelong ambition of mine to write a book.

I was challenged by my partner in this, Ben Jones, to write some books on a series of topics. Some topics I might not necessarily know anything about. Yet that was the joy of being an author with this kind of non-fiction book. The task in hand is to immerse yourself in research and take all your learning into a new written format that would be easy to understand, easy to follow and easy to apply.

So this book started out as a test. A test to see if I could actually research the content, write a book, publish and launch a book. The biggest test though is that people would read the book, be inspired and take action from it - resulting in them achieving their goals.

So, I chose to write about the subject of self discipline and avoiding procrastination as it was something I was overcoming and constantly working on for myself.

I spent much of 2016 working on my own self discipline by consuming many of the books you will see referenced in this book. Those books changed my life, my mindset and my productivity levels. I worked alongside experts in self discipline and was able to apply their expertise and knowledge, principles and methods in so many areas of my life -

particularly my job (the one that paid the bills) working as freelance communications consultant. Yet the hilarious irony of this book is that actually, in the beginning, *I had no self discipline to write it.*

After three months of just talking about the book, a frustrated Ben (who is officially the world's greatest accountability partner) via video call in Thailand, set me a challenge to set aside an hour. In that hour, all I had to do was put pen to paper and outline the chapters of the book. Up until this point, every single idea for the book was stored... in my head.

Ben politely, but firmly, instructed me to empty my head of all the stuff I knew already and all the knowledge I already possessed and put into action when it came to self discipline. He virtually, via his laptop, on the other side of the world, held my hand and encouraged me to take that first tiny step. He stayed on the call with me, and was shocked to see that in just 45 minutes, not only had I brain dumped everything I knew in a mind map, but I'd written the chapter headings and outlined the sub headings too.

Then... do you know what happened? I saw it all laid out. My plan. My book. I appreciated that I had a lot of knowledge on the subject and a heck of a lot of real-world experience putting the knowledge into practice. I really was a little expert in all of this. I already applied so many of these self discipline principles in many areas of my life.

I got cross. With myself. I'd wasted 3 months. But, I drew an imaginary line underneath it all, cleared my diary and I mustered every fibre of self discipline I could and wrote the first draft of this book in just 3 days.

Self discipline is a work in progress for me. In the same way you need to go to the gym regularly to keep your muscle tone, or eat well to keep your weight down, I believe that self discipline and self development is like the gym for the mind. You have to commit to it, every day. The more you do, the easier it gets.

I will never profess to having all my stuff together in my head and my life. I run my own business and I do work round the clock. I balance this with being a mum to Blake who is 7 and very energetic and support my husband who has a demanding job he loves and clear career path. Like you, I'm busy. Really busy. But I make sure that I make time for self disciplined actions.

Time for me, time for myself, time to achieve my goals.

It's not been easy, but it has been so rewarding. Especially now writing this. I've appreciated and celebrated how far I've come and I'm excited for where your own self discipline journey could take you too.

I am absolutely thrilled that you have purchased this book and given yourself a little time to learn more about how to flex that self discipline muscle and make more time and in turn create even more energy to achieve your own goals.

Free Online Self Discipline Course

I have seen first hand the power of online learning when it comes to self development and I wanted to create something for you, my reader, which will assist you in creating profound change and inspire you into action. I have therefore written and produced a highly valuable 10 day habit building programme alongside the book and encourage you to sign up to the online self discipline course.

The programme is delivered to your email inbox each morning over a 10 day period to help you establish winning habits, traits and build unbreakable self discipline.

Simply visit www.mindandbodyworld.com/selfdiscipline to register your details and the first email will be with you the following day at 6am.

To accompany this book, we have also created a dedicated Facebook group here: www.bit.do/selfdisciplinefacebook

Connect with like minded individuals who are also choosing to follow the steps outlined in this book. Get yourself an accountability partner, share stories, compare learning and celebrate your action steps and wins towards your goals.

For further reading, publications and additional resources, please visit www.mindandbodyworld.com

Gemma Ray

Author - Self Discipline: A How-To Guide to Stop Procrastination and Achieve Your Goals in 10 Steps

Gemma Ray

Introduction Part One

Self discipline

ˌsɛlfˈdɪsəplɪn/

noun

1. the ability to control one's feelings and overcome one's weaknesses.
   "his observance of his diet was a show of tremendous willpower and self discipline"

Self discipline. What is it exactly and why is it so important?

Self discipline is having the get up and go to complete daily positive actions in your life that lead to inner happiness, the sense of being in control and feeling content.

You've come across this book to learn more about self discipline, which makes me hazard a guess that you might have felt like you're struggling in this area.

I'd like to reassure you that you DO have the capability to exercise self discipline. Everyone does. Self discipline is the reason we get up, get washed, brush our teeth and head to work. If we didn't have any self discipline at all, well we'd probably just turn into a festering potato wouldn't we? And a poor and unhygienic one at that.

I believe that self discipline is three tiered:

Habit

Motivation

Conscious Disciplined Actions

Conscious Disciplined Actions

Are the steps you take in order to achieve your goals and feel in control your weaknesses. These actions are the foundation stones, the repeated actions over time that lead to great things. At first, they don't feel easy. You have to perform them in a very conscious way where you're aware of their need to be completed, and it can feel painful and challenging at first.

Motivation

It is possible for conscious disciplined actions to change from something forced to something you love to do. This leads to a subtle change and you actually want to do it!

Imagine you start out on a health kick and go to the gym. The first few gym visits might take a lot of self discipline to get there. Yet, soon you notice the positive effects on your body and mind and you find that you WANT to go. You are gradually motivated to head to the gym to train.

Soon, once you've repeated enough of these daily actions, you're naturally motivated to continue the positive effects of the conscious self discipline action steps. The result? The process feels less forced and like an easy part of life.

Habit

Eventually, if you repeat your conscious disciplined actions with enough motivation and comfort that you find they slide into your daily routine with ease. They're so ingrained into your life, they're there to stay - they become habit.

So you start your gym regime, you notice the positive effects and you're more motivated to go and eventually it's second nature and you're on autopilot as you pack your gym bag and head there without a second thought.

No One-Size-Fits-All Model

The following chapters contain a lot of information and a lot of strategies when it comes to mastering self discipline. Some will contradict one another. That's not me being a hypocrite. In researching many different self discipline methods it has become evident that there is no one-size-fits-all model. You need to take what you need from this book. Be inspired, try things out, be realistic and know what would work for you and your individual personality.

I encourage you to be totally honest with yourself, accept responsibility for the choices you have made so far in your life, forgive yourself if you need to. Make notes. Scribble in the margins, add annotations on your Kindle or tablet, get a journal and make notes as you go. Or don't. That's cool too. Just promise you'll try some of these techniques, because I promise when you do, you will feel like you've got your shit together that little bit better.

The accompanying 10 day online coaching course will help you get to know yourself a little better and help you come up with an action plan of self discipline steps to help improve different areas of your life.

If you haven't yet registered for the 10 day online course, please visit www.mindandbodyworld.com/selfdiscipline

Introduction Part 2

Setting Your Goals

Goal

gəʊl/

noun
plural noun: **goals**
the object of a person's ambition or effort; an aim or desired result.
"he achieved his goal of becoming King of England"

Have you picked up this book with a specific goal in mind already or are you not sure what it is you're looking to accomplish?

If you aren't sure on your goal specifics, try this exercise out for size.

You will need pieces of paper, a simple list on your phone or tablet or if you're a visual person, you might want to use post-it notes.

The 100 List

Set aside some quiet time, ideally with no distractions and compile a list of 100 things you want to see, do, achieve or experience.

Your workbook as part of the 10 day online course contains the necessary format to complete this. If you haven't already done so, you can sign up to the valuable 10 day online coaching course here www.mindandbodyworld.com/selfdiscipline. The pre-work workbook sheet has a done-for-you structure for you to complete this assignment.

The first step is to write down your 100 goals which can be anything you desire. Now 100 seems a lot, I know. You aren't going to focus on all of them at the same time, you're just using this exercise to get clear on the things you're striving for right now at this point in your life. Don't be scared to think really big and aim high. Also don't forget about the small stuff too.

Maybe there are places you want to see, health improvements you want to make or material things you want to buy. Maybe you want to set up your own business, lose an amount of weight, reach a financial goal, build your own home or maybe you just want to do something small like improve your sleep.

Once you have your 100 list, go back through and categorise your wishes and goals into sections.

Are they to do with money, work, knowledge, adventure, health, family, hobbies, materialistic, etc.? Give them a colour code or a symbol so you can see at a glance which category your goals fall into. Create your own categories specific to you if you need to.

Have a look at which goals fall into which category. Is there a category that has more than others? Why do you think this is?

Assess your 100 list and pick out a top 10 that are the most important to you.

Then, when you've categorised them and picked your top 10, place them into time-specific boxes.

Which of these things on your final list of 10 things can you achieve:

- this week
- short term (within the next year)
- long term (within the next 5 years)
- lifetime
- any you might have completed already

Look at these final 10 and where they fit. What patterns do you see and notice?

From the final 10, shortlist them to 3 goals. Doesn't matter if they're short term or long term, these 3 goals are the ones I want you to focus on when reading this book.

Make a note of your 3 goals somewhere prominent you will see them. Maybe stick them on a noticeboard in your house. Pin them to the bathroom mirror so you can look at them every morning. Create a new screensaver for your phone with your top 3 goals in view.

Setting Your Smart Goals

Now you have your top 3 goals in mind, it's time to work on making them SMART.

Reading a book on self discipline then building action steps and habits to achieve your goals is pointless unless you have that right goal in mind.

Yet at the same time, *keeping a goal in your mind* is actually the very worst thing you can do.

Why?

A goal in the mind is *just a dream*. You can dream and wish and want all day long but until you start creating some action steps to work on, that dream and your success will not move off the first step of the goal ladder.

Many years ago I read a very famous book called 'The Secret' by Rhonda Byrne which promotes the power of The Law of Attraction and gratitude. You may have read it?

I consumed this book, and read all her follow-up work. I started practicing gratitude through journaling and even set up a successful Facebook group called 'The Attitude of Gratitude' to get others to join in and feel grateful about many aspects of their lives.

I felt happier the whole time. So did the other people who joined me in this daily practice. It was powerful in changing how I thought and felt and enabled me to see positives in negative situations.

It was hard to feel negative and hard-done by when I was being grateful for everything in my life multiple times each day. However, I really didn't achieve all I'd been hoping to.

One recurrent theme in all of Rhonda Byrne's books is *Ask. Believe. Receive.*

She encourages you to "**ask** the Universe" for what you want, "**believe** it to be true, and act as if it has already happened" and then to "**receive** all that you desire" from the Universe.

I practiced this for a couple of years. I made vision boards and meditated, visualising my goals in my mind. Some of my goals I did achieve. This simple practice had brought them into my consciousness and I was now aware of the steps I had to take, and I took them quite naturally.

Other goals fell by the wayside. A simple matter of daydreaming about them wasn't going to help me focus my efforts and create a plan.

That's why I believe the '*Ask. Believe. Receive*' message is flawed. It is no good keeping your goals as pictures in your mind or on a board. Your goals need a strategy and a plan.

I am a big believer that the right and more realistic formula for achieving your goals in this realistic plan:

- Ask
- Believe
- Devise an action plan of small steps towards your goal
- Action these steps every single day
- Achieve

How Do You Devise An Action Plan For Your Goals?

So we have your top 3 goals in mind. I encourage you to follow the SMART method when looking to devise a plan on how to achieve them. It will help you figure out exactly what you want and how to get there.

It follows this acronym:

S - Specific
M - Measurable
A - Attainable
R - Relevant
T - Timely

I'll outline each one individually and a set of helpful questions you can ask yourself when goal setting.

SMART GOAL SETTING - Specific

Getting specific with your goal will help you decide what it is you actually want to achieve. The more specific you can be with your goal outline, the bigger chance you have of achieving it.

Throughout this book I will pose various questions to you. These questions will appear with this word: >>>*Journal*<<<

It is a valuable exercise to get a notebook specifically for this book, and make notes as you read. You can answer the questions and discover your own truth and path this way.

>>> *Journal* <<<
The following questions may help you get specific:

- What do I want to accomplish?
- Why do I want to achieve this?
- What do I need to **stop** doing?
- What do I need to **start** doing?
- What are the challenges?

SMART GOAL SETTING - Measurable

There's nothing worse than having a goal in mind, working on it and then changing the goal posts once you're on your way. Knowing your end point and at what point to pop open the Champagne is vital for feeling a sense of achievement.

You'll need to provide evidence to yourself for this section and a clear checklist to refine exactly what it is that you want. Defining this section will make your goal crystal clear and easy to reach.

>>> *Journal* <<<

Questions to think about:

- How will I measure my progress?
- How will I know when I have achieved this goal?

SMART GOAL SETTING - Attainable

It really IS possible to take a goal that seems impossible, plan smart and go for it at all costs until we achieve it. However, sometimes we also need to be a little realistic. Do we have the time? Do we have the talent? Do we have the money? Do we have the effort required for every step of the journey?

This section will help you to weigh up the time, effort and other costs your goal will take against the profits and other obligations and priorities you have in life.

The last thing you want to do is bankrupt yourself or end up divorced because of a seemingly possible goal.

There is absolutely nothing wrong with dreaming big and aiming for the moon when it comes to goals. Just add in a pinch of reality here when answering the following questions:

>>> *Journal* <<<

- How can this goal be accomplished?
- What are the logical steps I can take?

SMART GOAL SETTING - Relevant

This one requires a lot of soul searching and thought. Is reaching this goal relevant to you or someone or something else?

Are you going for this for the right reasons? Will this make you and your family happier? Healthier?

Are you just going for this to show off, or for the validation and acceptance of others? Or is this something that truly makes your heart sing and gives you the tingles just thinking about it?

If you are lacking in certain skills or qualifications you can retrain. If you lack resources or finances, you can create a strategy to look for them and secure them.

If you are lacking in time, with family commitments then this is the section to explore that and what it will look like.

Do you really want to be famous, jetting round the world on your speaking tour, with three kids at home and a partner who hasn't seen you for weeks?

>>> *Journal* <<<
Questions to ask yourself and the relevance of this goal:

- Is this a worthwhile goal?
- Is this the right time in my life?
- Do I have the necessary resources to accomplish this goal?
- Is this goal in line with my long-term objectives?
- How will this goal enhance my life?

SMART GOAL SETTING - Timely

Setting deadlines for yourself will turn your dreams into reality. Switching from dreaming to action requires a time sensitive plan and a deadline for yourself, your team or anyone else involved in your goal will be the difference between success and failure.

Keep a realistic timeline and keep it flexible too - just in case any curve balls come your way. On the flip side, there would be nothing worse than wasting the launch of a product or service by going at it too soon, before it is ready. You don't want to be killing yourself and burning everyone else out as you race towards the finish line.

Keep morale high and check in regularly on those involved in your goal, or get yourself an accountability buddy who is working on their own project to bounce ideas off. We'll explore that in more detail in step 3.

>>> *Journal* <<<
Timely questions to ask yourself:

- How long will it take to accomplish this goal?
- When is the completion date of this goal?
- When am I going to work on this goal?

1.1 Making goals SMART

Let's take three different goals and make them SMART in the following examples.

1) I want to lose weight
2) I want to be a millionaire
3) I want to become a qualified personal trainer

All three goals above are very vague and what we would refer to as 'passive' goals. Let's now make them SMART active goals.

1) I want to lose weight

S - Specific

What do I want to accomplish?
I want to lose at least 24lb of body fat.

Why do I want to achieve this?
Because none of my clothes fit me and I am not feeling good about myself.

What do I need to stop doing?
Eating junk food, eating takeaways, drinking sugary drinks, consuming too much alcohol, making excuses about the gym.

What do I need to start doing?
Drink 2 litres of water a day, reduce my sugary drinks consumption, change my alcohol from beer to spirits and mixers and work on reducing consumption, going to the gym 4 times a week.

What are the challenges?
Cravings for sugary sweets, not preparing food in advance and eating out, no motivation for the gym, getting up too late.

M - Measurable

How will I measure my progress?
I will check in with myself each week. I will weigh myself and take measurements every Monday and take update pictures every four weeks.

How will I know when I have achieved this goal?

When I have lost 24lbs.

A - Attainable

How can this goal be accomplished?
By drinking water every day, reducing sugary drinks, reducing alcohol, going to the gym, getting up earlier, pushing myself harder when exercising.

What are the logical steps I can take?
- I will prep my meals in advance to keep me on track
- I will buy myself a new water bottle and keep it with me
- I will install an app to track my water consumption
- I will aim for 10,000 steps each day on my Fitbit
- I will diarise my gym sessions every week in advance
- I will ask my friend to become my gym buddy and train with me
- I will keep track of my progress each week

R - Relevant

Is this a worthwhile goal?
Yes, I will feel healthier, look better and have more energy for other areas of my life. It will improve my self-confidence and prove to me that I can achieve my goals.

Is this the right time?
Yes, there is no time like the present to work on my health and well-being.

Do I have the necessary resources to accomplish this goal?
Yes, I have a gym membership but I could do research into home and bodyweight workouts I can do from anywhere so that I continue to train.

Is this goal in line with my long-term objectives?

Yes, long term I want to be as healthy as possible to live a long and happy life.

T - Timely

How long will it take to accomplish this goal?

I will aim for 2lb per week so 12 weeks.

When is the completion date of this goal?

12 weeks from now.

When am I going to work on this goal?

Every day with drinking water and nutrition and four times a week for the gym.

2) I want to be a millionaire

S - Specific

What do I want to accomplish?

I want to earn a million dollars a year by creating a new app to help people with time management.

Why do I want to achieve this?

Because I believe I can and I know that this will help so many people to also achieve their goals.

What do I need to stop doing?

Having self-doubt, believing that I "don't know enough", procrastinating, worrying about the finances.

What do I need to start doing?
Create a sustainable daily routine that factors in time to work on the app development. Recruit an investor to help with the finances. Recruit another developer to create the app.

What are the challenges?
Finances and not having enough investment. My own anxiety and overwhelm. My day-to-day business responsibilities as this currently pays the bills and is a priority.

M - Measurable

How will I measure my progress?
I will get myself an accountability buddy and organise regular check ins and conversations to keep me on track with my goal.

I will create a launch timeline, scheduling regular meetings and analysis of our progress.

How will I know when I have achieved this goal?
When my app is generating $84,000 dollars in paid revenue per month.

A - Attainable

How can this goal be accomplished?
By creating a comprehensive strategy from idea development to implementation, marketing to maintenance.

By recruiting investors to assist financially on the project.

By identifying which team members can be responsible for each section.

By creating team communication and benchmarks for each stage using software like Slack, Trello or Evernote.

What are the logistical steps I can take?
- I will create a full outline of the app, its content and how it works.
- I will create a presentation about the inner workings of the app to present to investors.
- I will recruit an accountability buddy to keep me on track with my goals and bounce ideas off.
- I will recruit another developer to share the workload and create the app software.
- I will plan and write a book about time management alongside the app to help promote the app.
- I will recruit copywriters to create valuable content on time management for social media and blogs to help drive traffic towards downloading the app once developed.

R - Relevant

Is this a worthwhile goal?
Yes, this is something I have wanted to achieve for a long time and will enable me to help many people at once while creating a passive income.

Is this the right time?
Yes, there are many apps on the market. I have downloaded most of them and they fall short in terms of keeping me on track. I believe I have the right model to help people not only establish effective time management, but maintain it.

Do I have the necessary resources to accomplish this goal?
I have around 75% of the resources to achieve this goal at present with my own knowledge, research and content. I am lacking in funding and know

with time constraints that I should consider hiring another developer to move the project along quicker.

Is this goal in line with my long-term objectives?
Yes, my long-term objective is to earn $1m a year and this goal will help me achieve that.

T - Timely

How long will it take to accomplish this goal?
I will aim to set up the app in one year and achieve my revenue income goal within the next 5 years.

When is the completion date of this goal?
One year from now for the app, and five years from now for the financial goal.

When am I going to work on this goal?
I am going to use the first 2 hours of my day to work on this goal every single weekday and plan a whole day once a month on a weekend to work on this goal.

This will give me a minimum of 48 hours per month to work on this goal.

3) I want to become a personal trainer

S - Specific

What do I want to accomplish?
I want to be a highly successful qualified personal trainer.

Why do I want to achieve this?

Because I am unhappy and unfulfilled in my current role and I have wanted a career change for a long time.

What do I need to stop doing?

Wasting time on social media, worrying about paying the bills, delaying starting my training.

What do I need to start doing?

Commit to a training course, decide on a timescale for study, diary in practice and theory study.

What are the challenges?

Studying while working full time.

M - Measurable

How will I measure my progress?

I will check in with myself each week to assess how my study has gone. I will ask a close friend to be someone I can answer to and who I will tell when I have completed study and assignments.

How will I know when I have achieved this goal?

When I achieve my qualification, leave my job to become a personal trainer AND have a diary full of paying clients.

A - Attainable

How can this goal be accomplished?

By committing time to study and practice.

What are the logistical steps I can take?

- I will get up 1 hour earlier every day to study over breakfast and coffee.

- I will dedicate 3 hours each Saturday and Sunday morning to my study or practical learning in the gym.
- I will regularly assess myself and my progress, making sure I am not procrastinating and falling behind.
- I will contact personal trainers I know and ask to shadow them for a day or two.
- I will book annual leave and book in a time to shadow other personal trainers.
- I will start to make contact with gyms and local personal trainer companies to secure a role at the end of my training.
- I will look into marketing for fitness professionals to help me market myself once I am qualified.

R - Relevant

Is this a worthwhile goal?
Yes, I want a career change and I have always wanted to do this.

Is this the right time?
Yes, I am not getting any younger and I am very unhappy in my current job.

Do I have the necessary resources to accomplish this goal?
Yes, I have signed up to the course, I have my course materials and study and there is a wealth of information out there for me to read up on in addition to my course study.

Is this goal in line with my long-term objectives?
Yes, I am very excited about a career that will not only fulfill me but keep me healthy and happy too.

T - Timely

How long will it take to accomplish this goal?
My course is three months long so I am to hand in my notice at work in 8 weeks time and have secured a position within a gym setting by the time my course finishes.

When is the completion date of this goal?
Three months from now.

When am I going to work on this goal?
Every morning over breakfast, bedtime reading on evenings where I have more free time and 3 hours every Saturday and Sunday for reading and practical study.

I will also book annual leave before I leave my job to shadow other fitness professionals and seek their knowledge and guidance.

1.2 Focus on the positive

One thing that is vital when setting SMART goals is to formulate a positive plan of action that is brimming with positivity and only positive action steps. Outline what you will focus ON doing, rather than setting plans that put your focus and your awareness on NOT DOING certain things .

For example, instead of telling yourself that you will 'stop feeling overwhelmed', you can flip that and instead say 'create a daily focused action plan'.

Another example, instead of telling yourself 'tomorrow I will stop eating chocolate', you can flip it to a positive and productive behaviour instead and say 'tomorrow I will drink more water and take more fruit for my snack'.

1.3 Assess along the way

Make sure you take time to assess your goals along the way. At the start of any SMART goal process you might want to diarise specific time slots over the course of the goal duration to check in with yourself.

For example if you have given yourself a 12 week timeframe for your goal, pop a reminder in your diary every week or two weeks to assess how you are doing with your goal and if you are working on the right things at that time to move you forward.

Do those diary reminders now. In advance. They make a difference.

We will talk about assessing your progress and checking in on yourself throughout your goal journey in more depth in Step 8.

1.4 Know when to stop and reward

Planning in rewards and moments to celebrate your goal achievements are very important. In Shawn Acor's brilliant book, The Happiness Advantage, and subsequent TED talk on this subject, Shawn discovers that human beings make themselves miserable when they change their pre-set goal posts that define success.

As a Harvard professor in Positive Psychology, Shawn has helped people all over the world to improve their productivity and performance by over 30%.

How? He focused on happiness. His work took him to over 42 countries and working within schools and companies all over the world. Each place he went, he asked his crowd what was the formula for happiness that had been taught to them from childhood? The answer was usually the same:

Work hard = be successful = be happy

But this formula is flawed and broken. For every time we achieve success, we then move the goalposts and expect happiness to be on the other side of that. So effectively we are always chasing happiness and never feel fulfilled.

Let's use someone working in a sales role as an example of this.

If Jeff hits his sales target for the last quarter, his target for the next quarter gets increased. That's just the way of the sales world. Yet this is extremely frustrating for Jeff. One way this is combatted is by commission or a sales bonus; Jeff is financially rewarded for achieving his target (Yet remember, it isn't all about money) however that target changes constantly and the job gets harder and harder with every new goal post that is changed and repositioned.

Along the way of your goal journey, it is important to stop and assess every micro success. This will keep you motivated and fuel to onwards to continue with the daily steps needed to achieve your goal.

Once you have set the end goal and the time limit - STICK TO IT! If you said you wanted to lose 10lb, then celebrate when you lose 10lb! Don't decide that it isn't enough and that you now actually want to lose 10lb more.

You might want to treat yourself when you reach these goals, a little like Jeff's bonus. You might treat yourself to a new outfit if you lose a dress size, or a mini break if you achieve sales of $3000 a month for example.

Just know what it is you're achieving and make sure you have a plan to celebrate it when you get there.

We go into more depth on this in Chapter 9.

2.1 Getting clear on what you want

I've been writing this during downtime while watching a friend of mine, Sheldon Oscar, compete in the Miami Pro bodybuilding show.

It's the first time he's done something like this. At 33 years of age, Sheldon has spent the last 8 years working as a fitness coach and before that, had hopes of competing as a professional boxer. Sadly, the boxing career wasn't to be and a hand injury and subsequent operation meant he had to hang up his gloves for good. Yet that ingrained desire and drive to compete, to win, has never really left him.

Sheldon decided to try out for a bodybuilding show to have some element of healthy competition in his life again, now that his professional boxing career is no more. He said that he would use the training months to compete with himself, and then on the day of the show it would feel like a boxing match; him against his opponents (the other competitors on stage).

He competes with himself because of a deep-rooted desire to prove to nobody but himself that he has got what it takes. Because he's so clear on what he wants, the process has been relatively easy - even when restricting his calorie intake as drastically as he did. His clarity on his goal, coupled with his self discipline and daily habits meant he emerged victorious and not only won his category, but the overall show too.

It was wonderful inspiration for me, and timely when writing this book. There were over 150 people; men and women on that bodybuilding stage this weekend who all possessed the most incredible levels of self discipline and self control – particularly around food and training.

Each bodybuilding competitor on that stage was in the most impressive physical condition and had worked hard for months, sometimes years, to get to their goal. Their consistent daily habits in terms of food and training paid off on the day.

I overheard one woman at thecompetition who was struggling mentally with the final show day stress. All she could talk about was her need for doughnuts at the end of the day. She also said "I'll show them. Who's had the last laugh now?!". She then started a conversation with her friends and it turned out that this woman was bullied as a child for being overweight. This was the drive that had got her in the competition-ready muscular shape she was in. I looked on, feeling sad as I realised she was was all smiles for the camera getting her latest status updates out there, yet when the lens was away from her face, she looked entirely miserable!

So with the two scenarios above, which one is clear on their '**why**' and which one is possibly attempting this for the wrong reasons?

I'm not saying that the woman couldn't go out there and give it her all, achieving an amazing goal, but is it really the right reason? If you're looking to achieve a goal to get a sense of validation, or please someone else, or to fight back against demons from your past, is that goal true to you? And true to you as a person here and now in this present moment?

2.2 Being honest about why you want it

Knowing the reason behind your motivation to do something, or achieve a goal is a challenge, but can give you a great indication whether you will follow through with your goal or not.

After all, if you're not working towards a goal for the right reasons, you're more likely to forget about it, drop it, or worse - hate the process!
So it's time to get ridiculously honest with yourself.

>>> *Journal* <<<
Take a minute to ask yourself the following questions:

- What is my driving force behind this goal?
- How will this goal positively impact my life?
- How will this goal negatively impact my life?
- What will I need to give up in my life to achieve this goal?
- Am I prepared to do that?
- What will I need to add into my life to achieve this goal?
- What do those I love think of this goal?
- Is this goal for me and me only, or am I really doing this to please/impress someone else?
- How will my life change once I have reached this goal?

Have a good look back at your answers and see what you said to yourself. If you feel like this goal truly is for you, and you know this will positively impact your life, then it is time to embark on those self discipline hacks and habits to get you there.

Step 1

Establishing Your Solid Morning Routine

"You will never change your life until you change something you do daily. The secret of your success is found in your daily routine."
– Unknown (Stolen from Instagram!)

"Gemma you can't just tell people to get up early. Nobody wants to get up early. We need to tell people why it is so powerful and works, and let them decide whether it is worth getting up early for."

Said Ben. My book buddy (you'll hear more about how our little accountability buddy arrangement works in Step 5 – Ways to Stay Accountable).

Ben was right. The first draft of this chapter basically told you to get up early and follow a morning routine. Which I will still tell you about in a minute. First I want to let you in on a secret.

The secret is, it's *no secret* that any book, podcast, article or interview with a successful CEO, entrepreneur, innovator that you listen to or read often says the same thing when asked that same question about the secret of their success. It wasn't overnight, it wasn't handed to them on a plate, they worked for it and they worked hard. The likes of Robin Sharma, Tony Robbins, Oprah Winfrey they all belong to the same club.

A club? There's a secret club you say? How do I get in? You *can. Anyone can*. It's the early morning club. But one with a conscious set of self discipline actions so powerful, they can literally change your life.

On New Year's Day 2016, I read an article from the New York Times about a journalist who had read two books that had changed her life.

The first was The Life Changing Magic of Tidying Up by Marie Kondo and the second Hal Elrod's The Miracle Morning.

The Life Changing Magic of Tidying Up is a manual on how to get rid of clutter in your life, stop buying stuff you don't need and find joy in everything you own.

The Miracle Morning is a manual on how to get up early and complete six different tasks in six specific categories to help you level up your life.

This woman in the article stood looking lithe and shiny in skin and hair, draped smugly across the furniture of her clean, organised, minimalist and calming home.

She'd picked up both books the year before and had been following both manuals for a whole year. The article was her sharing the results of living life by the two manuals.

She told tales of her financial triumphs, how she'd saved thousands by not buying stuff to clutter her home. She wrote in beautiful heartfelt prose about the wonders of her mornings thanks to Hal Elrod's methods and how she felt like a new person, in a permanent zen-like mode of stress free wonderfulness. I was hooked on her every word. How the hell had she done this?

And then the biggest shock of all. Right there, at the end of the article, there she was, pictured with her two boys. Two twin toddler boys. She oozed that super mum smug look from every freshly moisturised pore.

I put the article down. Looked at my absolute tip of a house, my muffin top, my overdraft and I hated that bitch. But I wanted her life. I wanted it all.

I downloaded both books. As it was New Year I had a week off work and instead of bingeing on box sets and chocolate selection boxes, I consumed every word. I watched YouTube tutorials and I read blog after blog on the art of tidying and the magic of waking up early.

By the time I went back to work a week later, my house was unrecognisable, and clutter free. I'd lost half a stone. I'd sold a load of stuff on eBay and was back in the black.

The biggest difference was how I felt and how I behaved in a morning. I was getting up to do the routine around 90 minutes earlier than I had been.

The concept of Hal Elrod's Miracle Morning is you follow six specific actions in a morning using the easy-to-remember acronym: SAVERS

It stands for

S – Silence
Meditating, or praying or sitting in silence.
I started to meditate and downloaded some meditation apps.

A – Affirmation
Affirming to yourself something positive about yourself. I wrote mine down and had a variety of really positive phrases I took the time to say to myself. One that I repeat daily (for 18 months) was "I am working less and earning more."

V – Visualisation

Visualising your goals or things you want to achieve. In that first week I used this part of the routine to visualise myself being mindful over food, loving my body and being grateful for my health.

E – Exercise

I changed this up a bit each day. One day I found a yoga routine on YouTube, one day I walked the dogs, and one day I went to the gym to a spin class.

R – Reading

I was reading both books at every opportunity that week, and also reading blogs and other articles on the subject of morning routines and reducing clutter.

S – Scribe

I started my own Bullet Journal. I started to write about things I was grateful for again. It's something I'd done in the past and I was once again feeling so happy and positive every morning by focusing on the wonderful things in my life.

The Miracle Morning allowed me to take responsibility for my own actions and turn mornings into a productive powerhouse of activity that empowered me to change my whole life.

You see, up until that point I'd convinced myself that I was not a 'morning person' and there's no way I could get up early every day. I'd had a job in my early twenties as a radio presenter on the breakfast shift of 97.4 Rock FM, a radio station in Preston. The job required me to get up at 5am. I struggled for years and years to get up and would rush in with seconds to spare before we went live. I would tell everyone who listened how exhausted I was all the time, and even likened my early mornings to feeling like I had "constant jetlag".

I can now tell you that was fabricated and in my own head.

I allowed myself to constantly complain about tiredness and tell myself that I COULDN'T get up on time every day. It actually got so bad that I referred myself to a sleep disorder centre, convinced there was something medically wrong with me.

Within 24 hours of reading The Miracle Morning, I couldn't believe I was getting up 90 mins earlier than I usually would be, with ease.

Why? I took responsibility for my own thoughts and I told myself I *could*.

Funny that.

I recommend The Miracle Moring to so many people and it's usually met with a "oh I honestly can't get up in a morning" response. Honestly though, I promise you can learn to love mornings.

You have to be a little bit of a crazy person to be able to all of a sudden start getting up hours earlier than you used to. I'm lucky, I am that crazy all or nothing personality so it really worked for me. The trick is finding what works for you.

The Purpose Of The Morning Routine

Your morning routine is created to make your life easier and help you start your day on the right foot.

If you have time for yourself in the morning and the things that will help energise you, you will start your day with a spring in your step and feel in control.

Before I focused on my routine before the working day started, my mornings were insane.

My husband leaves for work at 7am and I'd just sleep in. I'd set multiple alarms in different places around the house and I'd sleep through them all. Eventually I'd wake from my slumber and then run around like a woman possessed to get me and my son ready, and then off to school on time. It was horrible. Stressful and full of me shouting – especially at my son who was only just 5 years old at this point.

I wasn't proud of my behaviour and I knew it was not his fault at all. I was screaming at him to put socks on or hurry up eating his breakfast, but he's just a kid with no concept of time and he's my responsibility. I'd shout and stress from the moment I opened my eyes. I'd get him into school, late of course, and then I'd have to sprint, not run but sprint, often in heels, to get to my train on time. I would often go to work in tears.

Something had to change.

I found the morning routine and my life did change. Yours can too if your morning sounds even a smidge as stressful as mine did.

Starting Your Own Morning Routine

If you aren't an all or nothing weirdo like me, I'd recommend starting small when starting your morning routine.

You're more likely to stick to something if you start small and work your way up. Go all in straight away and you'll just give up and go back to old and comfortable habits.

So to get out of that comfort zone, think about the following concept and fill in the specific morning routine section in the workbook as part of the online course. If you haven't subscribed for that yet, please visit www.mindandbodyworld.com/selfdiscipline

What Does Your Ideal Morning Look Like?

Think about your mornings and the things you enjoy doing, or the things you know you could incorporate into your life that will benefit you. Exercise, meditation, keeping a gratitude journal, eating a healthy breakfast.

Now let's start with 5 minutes only.

If you've woken up later than ever, the proverbial has hit the fan, what one thing can you do in minutes or seconds that will help your day go better?

Mine is make a proper coffee and while it's pouring (takes 1 min 31 seconds - I timed it!) I can take some really deep breaths and I can stretch. Now that would make all the difference to my mornings. I love a cup of coffee to start my day and calming myself with some deep breathing. Stretching my arms and core is better than doing nothing at all and staying in a stressed state, and it takes mere minutes.

What could you do in 5 minutes that would help you feel centered, feel in control and feel like you've reclaimed the morning? Something that will put you on the right foot for the day, even if it only takes less than five minutes?

I asked friends and family for help with this one and here's some of their suggestions for five minute actions in a morning:

- The conscious choice to know that I don't have the time to check any of my notifications on my phone, put it by the door and focus on getting ready
- Putting on my makeup and a pair of heels
- A quick yoga sequence
- 10 jumping jacks
- A 5 minute meditation
- Saying aloud three things I am grateful for
- Sitting still for five minutes and visualising a smooth and stress free morning with no traffic!
- Stroking my dog
- Having a really quick cold shower to invigorate me and wake me up properly so I'll move quick and get out on time
- Putting on my favourite song and dancing like crazy
- Reading an inspirational quote
- Adult colouring book time
- Saying my prayers and asking God to help me have a great day

Now repeat this and create some actions and activities for your morning if you had:

- 15 minutes available
- 30 minutes available
- 45 minutes available
- 60 minutes available
- 60+ minutes available

You can even use the above method to gradually train yourself to get up earlier. Start with setting your alarm 5 minutes earlier in the first week, 15 minutes in the second, 30 minutes in the third and so on.

Ideas For Your Morning Routine

A morning routine needs to be enjoyable for you personally, otherwise like anything, you won't stick to it. Consistency is the key here so carving out your own golden time in the morning doing stuff you love is worth it.

Read other titles like Tim Ferris' Tools of Titans or Tribe of Mentors or any blog about the morning routines of successful entrepreneurs, athletes and celebrities and a lot of the same things come up.

From these books, interviews and podcasts and my own experience, here's what I'd recommend personally to incorporate in a morning routine:

Meditation

Meditation or quiet reflection is a great way to get your brain to rest and listen to your own thoughts each morning. You can ask yourself deep questions and think of answers in meditation or mindfulness practice, or choose to sit in silence and reflect.

Download a meditation app that can take you through guided systematic meditations depending on your need. For example, if you suffer from anxiety there is an anxiety meditation package in the Headspace app which you can follow.

One app I love is Insight Timer. It is a free meditation app used by over 2 million people worldwide. You can choose a guided meditation on a range of subjects, or use the timed feature to sit in silence and meditate with the option of choosing humming, water or other sound effects in the background.

The trick with mindfulness or meditation is to allow thoughts to come in, honour them, and then let them go. Focus on your breathing and your body and sit in the moment.

If you practice this regularly you will see a huge shift in your motivation and decision-making becomes easier.

You will start to notice your emotions and responses more, you will ask yourself powerful questions (for we all have the answers within us) and you will feel more centred, calm and less stressed.

It is also a great time to just be still and be - devoid of the hustle and bustle of everyday life. If you commute to your job, have kids or a generally manic schedule you will start to relish these silent moments in a morning. Many people call this time 'golden hour' and they're not wrong.

Enjoy the early mornings.

Positive Affirmations

An affirmation is a declaration or statement that you make to affirm something.

Personal affirmations you repeat to yourself are extremely valuable and help you connect to what you want. Positive affirmations are short statements that are used to re-program your thought patterns and change the way you feel about things. They help you focus on goals, get rid of negative thoughts, change beliefs and program the subconscious mind.

Now, deciding on affirmations causes debate. Many will tell you to make these statements as if they have already happened or you believe them to be happening and true (even if they aren't). In this case, you would start an affirmation with "I am".

For example;

- I am powerful
- I am beautiful
- I am a size 8
- I am a champion
- I am smoke free
- I am strong and lean

Other professionals believe that stating affirmations with "I am" may not be believable for the person speaking the words and instead advise to start affirmations with "I intend to" or "I will".

Whether you use "I am..." or "I intend to...", include these elements when choosing the words for your affirmation:

Speaking in the present tense - If you are able to feel like this is happening in the here and now, that you will have or can be something then it is more likely to happen. Stating your affirmation in the future may just keep it there - in the future and out of reach.

Keep it positive - Affirmations should state what you want not what you don't want. Using positive sentences instead of negative will have powerful repercussions. If you don't want a situation, like you may want to stop smoking, instead of saying "I intend to stop smoking" say: "I am smoke free" or "I am a non-smoker".

Does it feel good? - Notice your emotions when you say your affirmations. Do they feel good? Do they bring up good feelings? Or do they make you feel worried and anxious? They should make you feel good, and you should believe in them strongly.

Other examples of affirmations could be:

The "I am" way…

- I am working less and earning more
- I am the world champion
- I am healthy and strong with muscle definition
- I am organised and productive
- I am a money magnet and money flows into my life effortlessly
- I am healthy and strong and live life to the fullest
- I refuse to bear a grudge on anyone. I forgive and love.
- I love who I am and am happy in my own skin.

The "I intend to" way…

- I intend to reduce my hours and spend more time with the children
- I intend to take responsibility for all my actions
- I intend to live with courage
- I intend to be self-assured and self-confident
- I intend to enjoy my life with enthusiasm
- I intend to have a positive attitude towards difficult circumstances
- I intend to let the people in my life know that they are important to me
- I intend to forgive myself lovingly for the mistakes I make
- I intend to live a fulfilling life and enrich other people's lives

Carrie Green who runs the highly successful Female Entrepreneur

Association has her own daily affirmation that starts a little different, but it makes you think!

I can, and I will. Watch me.

That's a good one for when you're striving for something that others might deem impossible.

Reciting Affirmations

Affirmations can be recited back to yourself or written down.

The most powerful way to recite affirmations is to speak them aloud to yourself while looking in a mirror. The mirror technique requires you to look yourself in the eye and say the affirmations out loud, speaking to your subconscious and conscious self. It is truly life-changing when this is performed. You cannot lie to yourself in the mirror and your affirmations will be burned into your subconscious, forcing you to live them out.

You could journal your affirmations or you could put them on cards or prominent places around your home so that you will see them regularly.

You can even purchase affirmation cards. Louise L Hay's Power Thought Cards are a great choice for this and very handy to have. If you're struggling for affirmation inspiration, you can draw a card from the deck and see if it fits with you and your own goals.

Visualising Your Goal Achievements

Dream it and you can become it!

So you have learned about affirmations but what about visualisation?

Imagining your goal statements and visualising yourself immersed in achieving your goal as if you've already succeeded can be a super powerful exercise.

Did you know? Your brain does not know the difference between what is real and what is imagined. It is the reason why a vivid dream can feel so real, and sometimes why you question past events and wonder if you have imagined them, or if they were reality.

With that in mind, visualising success is a very important and widely used tool to teach the brain what you want in life and form those neural pathways to make it happen.

Many professional athletes use positive psychology and visualisation to imagine the feeling of winning that Olympic gold, or scoring that winning goal. There is much money spent on the mental conditioning of professional athletes and visualisations play a huge role.

So, what do you want? By now you should know what your goal is.

>>>*Journal*<<<
With your goal in mind, take a moment, maybe at the end of your meditation to really visualise your situation as if it is already happening right now.

- What can you see?
- What can you hear?
- What can you smell?
- What can you taste?
- What do you look like?
- How do you feel?
- Where are you?

Remember all those tiny details and focus on that end goal. If you're looking to lose weight, how are you looking and feeling? What are you wearing? What are others saying about your success?

If you're looking for financial success, how much is on your bank statement? What are you able to buy now that you're financially successful? How much money do you have in your hands?

If you're aiming for that promotion at work, what does it feel like knowing you've achieved it? What is your new office like? What does your new suit or clothing feel and look like? How are you feeling and acting in your new role?

You can even use visualisations in your affirmation work. If you are making positive statements that you can imagine happening in the present, say it aloud to yourself, look in the mirror and then take a moment to visualise that it is already happening for you.

Going back to the brain for a minute, this is all relevant and powerful because if you visualise it for long enough, your brain will try to make it happen.

Your brain is scanning the environment every single second, and while itsprimary function is to keep you alive and safe, it also looks for opportunities.

If you're telling yourself every day that you want a promotion, your brain will look for those opportunities in your working life that can help you step up and make that visualisation a reality. An overheard conversation, an email, a way to prove yourself; your brain will bring these into your consciousness to align with all you have been visualising.

Get Your Blood Pumping!

Moving your body first thing in a morning fires up your brain, your blood flow and your muscles. After a night in bed, getting up and getting moving is a great way to start your day.

Getting it out of the way at the start of the day works really well for some people. You just do it and don't have to think about it! When researching this book, I came across people who swore by going to bed in their gym clothes, they just got up and got out. Before their brain had chance to argue back! That's one way of doing it.

Whatever you do, just get moving. Some people grab their trainers and head straight out for a run. Some go off for a swim, others do yoga. Some just complete some exercises at home and light stretches. You know your own abilities and limits, and the point is to just move and fire up your system.

Whatever you choose to do, the harder you can push yourself, the better. Exercise has been scientifically proven to improve lifestyle, mental health and reduce body fat among other amazing benefits.

Google Dr Wendy Suzuki's 2017 TED Talk about the immediate positive benefit of exercise on the brain for your mood and focus. (She also goes into detail about the protective benefits of exercise on the brain for conditions such as depression, dementia and other neurological conditions).

Learn/Read/Listen

How much new information do you learn everyday? The infinite amount of research and knowledge out there means you can self-teach absolutely anything these days.

Once you start on a self-development path, your eyes will be opened up to the multitude of life-changing and inspirational books/podcasts and online resources that will help motivate you and help you to excel in your chosen field as well as on a personal level.

In the book Slight Edge by Jeff Olson, (which is a great read by the way), he points out that if the average book is 300 pages long, if you were to read 10 pages of a book each day, you would read a book a month and that's 12 books a year.

Imagine how much extra knowledge and learning you could absorb by reading an extra 12 books in a year! Yet many of us see a book and think "Nah, haven't got time". In fact, kudos to you for getting this far in this book. It shows that you are someone who reads.

Of course reading is not limited to books. The internet is a wealth of valuable information. You may choose to read articles, blogs, stories online. It all counts.

Remember, just 10 pages, 10 minutes a day and all those extra books you could read. How much additional knowledge and self-growth could you stockpile in the course of a year?

Keeping a Journal

I think there's something so powerful about writing things down in your own handwriting.

As previously mentioned, some people choose to journal and write a daily diary. Others choose to write out their affirmations (see previous) and others choose to use the time to write out their intentions for the day: a to-do list of sorts.

Whichever way you choose to journal, it needn't take long and putting pen to paper, seeing your own goals written down in your own handwriting all helps cement that belief that you will, and *can* achieve your goal.

Play

It's not all work and no play in a morning. Make sure there's time to play. With your kids, your dog, your cat, your other half.

You can have an extra ten minutes building Lego with your kid.

You can take the dog out for a walk.

You can play that game online for a minute. If that's something you like to do.

How Long Should My Morning Routine Take?

This is personal to you and also might change as you increase the strength of your self discipline efforts.

You obviously still need to sleep and rest, and you may choose to start off really small as suggested earlier in the chapter. Start with 5 minutes and start small. Build it up and see how you get on.

Personally, I am up 90 minutes to 2 hours before the rest of my family and I choose to go to bed a little earlier to fit it all in. My life has changed for the better since I adopted this approach and my days are so productive and focused.

Help! I Can't Get Up!

Oh I hear you! Even now I still really struggle to get up on that first alarm. Even two years down the line of trying to be consistent with a morning routine and I STILL struggle. I have a few alarms dotted round the house, including a Lumie clock which emulates sunset and sunrise to trick my brain into getting up. It's particularly helpful during the dark winter months.

For me, there are a few things to help you get up in the morning:

Getting Up On Time – The Night Before Routine

For me, my morning routine starts the night before. I find if I do a deload of the day in my head or journal, it helps me go to bed and sleep quicker and also plan out the following day.

Journaling the events of the day is helpful as it feels like I'm emptying my head on paper. I also use the time to work out what I have coming up in the diary the next day and what my priorities are. Doing this helps me sometimes set that alarm a little earlier, or a little later and be more realistic about the time I have available the next day to achieve everything I've written down.

I find that there are often small 2/3 minute jobs that appear on this 'night before' list that I can tackle there and then. Sending that email, ordering that birthday present online, transferring a bit of money into the savings, making our lunches. Getting some of the small stuff off the list often feels like a big achievement and I'm winning before the night is over and the next morning has begun.

The Dress Rehearsal

If I've had a run of particularly rubbish mornings and I've not been able to get up, I actively visualise my morning by doing a night before 'dress rehearsal'. Bear with me on this one, it sounds absolutely mental but it works!

I lie down in my bed, and close my eyes pretending to be asleep. I visualise my alarm clock going off. I hold my phone or iPad in my hands, close my eyes and visualise the alarm time displaying my get up time. I picture myself holding this in my hands as I sit up and swing my legs out of bed. I visualise tapping the alarm STOP button as I rise out of bed and start to walk to my door.

I pick up my dressing gown, put it on and walk to the bathroom. I splash my face with cold water, look in the mirror and say "Morning! Well done for getting up!" to myself in my head. I then walk out of my bedroom, into the living room and stretch. (I told you I was mental!).

Sometimes I repeat this dress rehearsal process 2 or 3 times. I then find that in the morning, when the alarm goes off, I know EXACTLY what to do (even though I have done this routine many times before). The dress rehearsal reminds me of the process and just how easy it is. It is the choice to hit snooze or stop, and the action steps I take straight after to keep me awake.

The Night Time Meditation

With the dress rehearsal above, if I have a spare 5 minutes I'll try a quick meditation which incorporates the mantra "I love my mornings and waking up early." I try and do this before bed to put my mind in the right state to wake early. I also sometimes listen to subliminal recordings overnight (you can find these on YouTube) which help me wake up early.

Alarm Clocks From Hell

The number 1 way I get up early is using alarm clocks. I always have a minimum of two, sometimes more, but when I complete the dress rehearsal and meditation above, I usually get up on the first one and the rest act as insurance.

I write notes to myself on the phone and iPad that display as the alarm sounds. Sometimes I use inspirational quotes, sometimes I write some pretty lovely things to myself and other times I'm not so nice "Get up you lazy bitch" is one that is quite effective!

I have also downloaded many apps in my time to help me get up. Some of them required me to take a picture in a specific spot or complete maths puzzles to wake up. All were really good, but I find I get clever quite quickly and even in my dozy state I work out ways to override their deafening instructions.

Recently I've discovered the most hilarious and irritating alarm app called Carrot. It spits insults out at me along with using mind bending puzzles and instructions to silence its deafening fog-horn like shrill. It's one I highly recommend! Just make sure your phone is plugged in and you leave the app running, otherwise it does tend to fail.

Straight in the Shower

This last tip is really simple. There's nothing like the water from the shower over your face to wake you up first thing in the morning.

If I'm being exceptionally lazy and not getting up for my run of morning routines, I will set my alarm and place the phone in the shower cubicle (somewhere out the way of the taps). When that alarm goes off first thing, in the echoey chamber of the shower it actively enhances the volume of the alarm and shocks me into jumping out of bed.

I write a note on the alarm to say 'turn on the shower', moving the phone to the safety of the dry sideboard and I try and jump straight in. A few times it has been freezing cold and definitely given me a cool, crisp wake up but whether the water is warm or cold, there's nothing like a shower to get me feeling refreshed and ready for the day.

Making Mornings Work For You – Recap

Remember – start small! Start with just 5 minutes and what you could do in that time. Don't forget to fill in the specific morning routine section in the workbook as part of the online course.

If you haven't subscribed for that yet, please visit www.mindandbodyworld.com/selfdiscipline

Step 2

Make Your Health a Habit

"Your body isn't a temple. It is a home you will live in forever. Take care of it."

- Unknown

"Your health is your wealth" is a great thought provoking statement that is certainly true. You can have the flashiest car, the biggest house, the biggest bank account but none of it is as precious and important as the body you live in. It really is the only place you have to live.

The only certainty in life is death. Yet, figuratively speaking, the time when that happens can be extended due to a few factors.

I always start with this one early on, because no matter what your SMART goal may be, also creating some healthy habits is universally recognised as a pillar of success. If you're overweight, unhealthy, stressed or not sleeping then you're not going to be performing at your optimum levels.

Looking after your health is one of the fundamental habits that every goal-striving person should put first.

It is no good aiming for your first million pound business if you're not feeling brilliant, not sleeping, stressed to death and living a miserable existence in your own body.

Prioritising your health means you will perform at your best.

How many people do you know who are "too busy" to drink water during the day, or take a lunch break? Heck, you might even be one of those people yourself!

Nobody is ever too busy for their health. It is a bullshit statement and it just re-affirms the fact that you are putting yourself last and not understanding how important your health is. Without it you are nothing.

Women are terrible at putting themselves first. Especially those who have children. They prioritise everyone's needs above their own and end up exhausted and fed up.

The first healthy habit to adopt is to PUT YOURSELF AND YOUR HEALTH FIRST.

Surviving off coffee and takeaways as you slave away on your goal will most certainly have a detrimental effect on your cognition and your motivation.

If you want to remain super productive and with a laser-like focus at all times then the key to this is your health.

In this book and in our online course, we encourage you to seriously consider the following for the benefit of your health and performing at your optimum best.

1. Drink at least 2 litres of water a day
2. Make conscious food choices and opt for whole single ingredient foods
3. Move your body
4. Look after your mental health
5. Develop a strict sleep hygiene routine

So let's look at each in more depth.

1.   Drink 2 Litres of Water a Day

When looking at self discipline with health I start on the good old H20. Water is the elixir of life and one really simple key habit of well-being that produces such powerful results when consumed in the right quantities.

Our bodies are made up of over 60 percent water. Blood is 92 percent water, the brain and muscles around 75 percent water and bones around 22 percent water. See why drinking enough of it is important?

Water regulates your body temperature, lubricates joints, protects the spine and other tissues and also acts as the main mechanism for excreting toxins and waste from the body.

It is no surprise that when you don't drink enough water, it really does affect your cognition and performance. There are so many people who are dehydrated every single day and often hunger pangs are not signals that you need food, but signals that you are actually thirsty and dehydrated.

Did you know, a human being can survive around a month or more without eating food, but only a week or so without drinking water? Yes, it's THAT important.

By the time you feel thirsty, your body has lost over 1 percent of its total water. So, without further ado, right now is the time to go and grab a big cool glass of the good stuff.

That's right, stop reading this and go grab a glass of water now.

There's this big line here on purpose so you can come back and easily find your place in the book once you've knocked back some of that H2O goodness.

GO AND DRINK A GLASS OF WATER

Got a glass of water? Good. Right where were we? You were here.

With that taken care of, you should know that for men, the average MINIMUM amount of water you should consume a day is 3 litres and for women is 2.2 litres.

Nope, sodas and tea/coffee don't count. Herbal non-caffeinated teas do count towards your total water consumption and they are a much better alternative than too many caffeinated drinks.

And of course, if you can drink more - even better!

You also may need to up your fluid intake if you live in a hot climate, exercise often or have fever or diarrhea. Add in an additional 0.5 - 1 litre of water per day if you exercise, even more if you work out longer than an hour.

How To Drink More Water

Firstly, this is one habit that does take a few days to get used to. If you're not currently a regular water drinker you will find that frequent toilet trips will become quite annoying in the first few days of consuming water regularly. However, I can assure you that this becomes the norm after only a few short days and the trips will become less frequent.

Many people do struggle to drink enough water and to remember to drink. Water isn't exactly the most exciting of drinks and it is easy to forget. Here's some tips on how to increase your intake:

1) **Water on waking**

As SOON as you wake up in the morning, grab yourself a full pint of water and drink it in one go. You will be dehydrated after sleep and this is a great way to replenish those fluids.

It will help get your bowels moving and is also a good time to take your morning supplements like a good multi-vitamin, probiotic and Vitamin D if you aren't living somewhere particularly sunny.

2) **Water alarms**

Set alarms for water throughout the working day. If you work in an office, this is also a great way to break up your tasks and following the Pomodoro technique (we will touch on this later in Step 7) is a great opportunity to stretch your legs and grab a glass.

3) **Carry a bottle of the wet stuff**

Invest in a large water bottle and take it with you everywhere. There are even some bottles on the market today that link with your mobile device and can send you handy reminders to drink more water and track your daily intake.

4) **There's an app for that**

Track your water intake on a handy app. You could use MyFitnessPal and track your food there too, or on the iPhone under the Health tab there is a place to track your water. There are also many apps out there that are inbuilt with regular reminders to ensure you meet your daily water goals.

5) The return home routine

When you get home from work, make it a habit to set down your bag and keys, take off your shoes and head for a cool glass of water straight away. This will also help you to stop picking at food before you have eaten your evening meal and keep those hunger pangs at bay.

6) Evening meal

Before your evening meal, enjoy a glass of water. Again, this will not only replenish you but stop you from mistaking thirst for hunger and overeating.

7) Go herbal

Swap your coffee and teas for herbal non-caffeinated teas that will all go towards your daily water target.

8) Jazz it up

Jazz up your water - add in fruits such as a squeeze or wedges of lemon, lime, orange and herbs such as mint to infuse more flavours into your water.

2. Make Conscious Food Choices

We human beings love our food. From the moment we are born we learn that food = love, comfort and the feeling of being satisfied. It is no surprise that we turn to food in adulthood to fill a void and give us a kick and boost.

With our programming, it is ingrained in us to 'treat' and 'reward' with food. But does this really help us? Are the food choices you make with your meals hindering your goal success?

They say that abs are made in the kitchen. Speak to any fitness professional who will confirm that the secret to a magazine-cover physique lies in what you eat, *not* how hard you train. If your goal is not fitness orientated, this is still relevant as what you eat will fuel your performance and your cognition.

Sugar is now known to be more addictive than crack cocaine. Its availability in everything is shocking and it is having a detrimental effect on our brain function, body composition and our moods. It is no secret that junk foods laden with sugar, salt and trans fats affect digestion and energy.

Your body spends between 10 and 25 per cent of its total energy on digestion. Foods depleted of natural enzymes take even more energy to break down which can leave you sluggish exhausted and reaching for that 3pm pick me up when at your desk.

Think about it. When you eat your Thanksgiving or Christmas dinner, how do you feel afterwards? I bet if you're anything like me you will need to adjust your belt buckle and you'll probably have a little snooze on the sofa within an hour of eating.

In contrast, how do you feel after a mouth watering fresh salad? I bet the total opposite! The live enzymes in the fresh, uncooked foods help your body to break down and digest the food, rather than working against your digestive system.

So with nutrition in mind, it's time to assess what you eat, when you eat and how you eat.

You Are What You Eat

Think about your current nutrition and eating habits. How do your current eating habits affect you? Do you eat for performance? Or are you always in a carb coma?

What do you eat for breakfast? Does it set you up for the day? Or leave you snoozing on the train on the way into work? Do you EVEN eat breakfast?

What do you grab for lunch? Are you eating on the go? Or maybe not even paying attention what you eat and munching mindlessly at your desk?

What is for dinner? Are you so exhausted and overwhelmed that you're dialling for the nearest pizza? Or are you meal prepping in advance and coming home to a healthy and nutritious crock-pot dinner?

>>> *Journal* <<<
Using your notebook, take a minute to answer these questions:

Q: What could I incorporate more of in my diet?

Q: What could I eat less of in my diet that doesn't serve me well?

The Whole Foods Approach

So that lean piece of meat, greens, rice and homemade salsa is going to be much more nutrient dense than the pre-packaged and processed burger and fries you're considering eating.

Eating fresh foods as often as possible will help fuel you for performance. Processed foods with long shelf life, added preservatives and chemicals are doing us no favours!

When you go shopping take a careful note of labels. If it has many ingredients and names you can't pronounce, coupled with a best before end date that's well into the future…avoid! Your brain's performance and your waistline will thank you for it!

Finding What Works For You

I advocate a single ingredient food approach here because if you've ever embarked on any healthy eating or nutrition change and incorporated more of this into your life, you will have noticed how it does make you feel more energised and helps you focus.

However, it's about finding a plan of eating that works for you, what you like to eat and how you live. So whether that's paleo, vegan, ketogenic, a slimming club points method, intermittent fasting etc (the list goes on) find what works and stick to it.

Food Diary

It's time for another little dose of honesty. The only way you can move forward with your nutrition is to assess where you are right now, draw a line in the sand and move on.

So, think back to what you have eaten in the last three days. There is a copy of this table in the workbook that accompanies the online course.

Today

Meal	Breakfast	Lunch	Dinner
What did you eat?	Breakfast panini		
Why did you choose this?	I got it from Starbucks in a rush		
How did it taste?	It was nice but a bit rubbery		
How did you feel after you'd eaten it?	Sluggish and it gave me gas		
Could you have made a better choice? If so, what was available?	Yes, I could've eaten bran at home, or chosen porridge		

Yesterday

Meal	Breakfast	Lunch	Dinner
What did you eat?			
Why did you choose this?			
How did it taste?			
How did you feel after you'd eaten it?			
Could you have made a better choice? If so, what was available?			

2 Days Ago

Meal	Breakfast	Lunch	Dinner
What did you eat?			
Why did you choose this?			
How did it taste?			
How did you feel after you'd eaten it?			
Could you have made a better choice? If so, what was available?			

3. Move Your Body

Exercise is the key to physical and mental performance. You know yourself, if you participate in a healthy regime which includes exercise you enjoy, it creates a ripple effect of positive change. You have more energy, you automatically make better food choices, your body composition can change.

So how do you move your body right now? Truthfully? If you currently regularly participate in sporting activities - good on you!

If you don't move your body at present, and particularly if you work in a sedentary role, how can you increase your physical activity for the good of your health and well-being?

Is there an activity that you loved to participate in, as a child, that you could pick up again in adulthood? Did you dance? Do gymnastics? Boxing? Running? There are a multitude of sporting classes out there, and also more gentle and spiritual activities such as yoga or pilates that are effective and challenging.

What could you do for your body? Answer that question, plan in the time and DO IT! Seriously, what is your excuse?

4. Look After Your Mental Health

Mental health is finally being recognised as a growing global health challenge and more and more people are taking it seriously.

Anxiety and depression are the most common mental health disorders in the UK, with 8.2 million cases of anxiety in the UK reported in 2013 and over 19% of the population recorded as suffering with depression in 2014.

That is a massive one in FIVE people!

Now depression and anxiety will not go away with a magic wand, words of encouragement or medication. Depression and anxiety are complex, I am no doctor and not here to play down these serious conditions.

I have been through periods of depression and I continue to experience anxiety. I have sought professional help and coaching for both and I'm pleased to report that it has been a huge help.

Here's some of my strategies I have been encouraged to adopt by professionals. These techniques took a lot of self discipline to try, when I was feeling low or down, but they truly made a difference. As per the morning routine chapter, I incorporated a lot of the following techniques into my morning to help me shape my mood and internal thoughts for the day ahead.

Meditation - whether silent or guided, meditation is one of the most effective ways to quiet a worrying mind and help someone to feel empowered to make the right decisions to feel better.

There are apps on them market including Calm and Headspace which can help you to relax, breathe deep and find the answers within to tackle your worries and problems. Insight Timer is another great meditation app that I recommend and it's free.

Journal - recording your thoughts and feelings in a journal, plus the act of actually putting pen to paper can help your mental health tremendously. Instead of having a head full of worries, you can offload your worries in writing and begin to address them.

Deep breathing techniques - taking a deep intake of breath is extremely calming and keeps you centred. Try it now. Take in a deep breath, hold it for a count of 8 and then breathe out for a count of 8. It will instantly make you feel more calm and in control. If you do suffer from anxiety it is a technique you may have been taught to instantly calm yourself.

Breathe by Dr Belisa Vranich is a good structured book on improving breathing. It is a 14 day guide on actively improving the way you breathe.

There's also the Wim Hoff method which is more extreme and also involves freezing cold showers. I've tried it! It was intense, but I could definitely see how it could help shock and calm the system. A few of my friends who work in fitness follow his methods and report that they love it as part of their routine.

Asking for help or reaching out – this was certainly the hardest thing for me to adopt but reaching out to others and being honest about my feelings really helped. I have a handful of friends who know my battles with depression and anxiety and being able to seek their advice, words of comfort or just have a friendly and understanding voice on the end of the phone was life changing.

When I was at my lowest, I didn't really want to communicate with anyone and I would shut myself away for long periods of time. Luckily, I have friends who have been through the same mental health challenges who were able to recognise my behaviour and coax me into talking. The more I talked about it, the easier it became to address how I was feeling and move on and out of feeling down.

It still takes a lot of effort to ask for help or just someone to talk to. I often feel ashamed when the periods of feeling down hit me, but the more I've reached out, the easier it is to just say "Hey, I'm struggling a bit at the moment, do you fancy a catch up?" Sitting in my own negativity has never been productive and getting out of it by sending that one small message has been so brilliant in getting me back on track.

Treating yourself - in this modern world of hustling and grinding it is easy to neglect your own self-care. Treats, rewards and perks can help cheer you up.

This could be setting aside time for an activity you adore, treating yourself to a massage, a new outfit, a relaxing spa day or a night out with friends. Whatever it is, make time to honour and love yourself with some treats.

I find having things to look forward to is very beneficial to keeping those down days at bay.

5. Develop a Strict Sleep Routine

Sleep is so important and vital to our well-being. Not enough sleep can have a negative impact on your health and well-being so it is time to implement some rest and recovery strategies.

On average, how much sleep do you get each night at present?

>>> *Journal* <<<

_____ Hours

And how many of the following good sleep habits do you already adopt in your daily routine?:

- No caffeine drinks after 4pm
- Bath before bed
- No electronic equipment 1 hour before bed (TV, PlayStation, iPad,

phone, Kindle)

- Journal and empty head of 'to do' list 1 hour before bed
- Light elimination (my bedroom is dark)
- Hydrate before bed
- Go to bed at a time to get at least 6-8 hours of quality sleep

Question for your journal:

>>>*Journal*<<<
What will I commit to, to make quality sleep a priority in my life?

A side note on food addiction:

After writing the first draft of this book, I thought about deleting this chapter all together as food is something I personally struggle with.

In my work as a copywriter, I've written for personal trainers, nutritionists and health coaches for many years. I feel like I have so much stored knowledge of many forms of eating and diets. I've written articles and eBooks on paleo, flexible dieting, IIFYM, ketogenic, veganism, raw foods, low carb, carb cycling, juicing, counting points...the list goes on.

Yet, I felt like a complete fraud writing a book including chapters on what to eat, when I was stuck in a spiral of compulsive eating and would binge on junk foods at every opportunity.

I have noticed that I eat my emotions - many people do! I eat when I'm happy, I eat when I'm sad and often I don't have the self discipline to stop.

I knew it had become a problem in my life and after a failed attempt at getting my blood sugar under control with my diet, I came across Overeaters Anonymous, an organisation linked to Alcoholics Anonymous. I have embarked on a program of recovery from my food addiction. Recovery sounds like a big and serious word to describe this, but my self discipline around food had disappeared and it was making me miserable. People were noticing and I got honest with myself about my secret eating and hidden stash of junk foods.

Now I have embarked on the Overeaters Anonymous program, I am enjoying getting to the root of my food addiction and learning more about myself and the reasons why I compulsively eat. I am feeling more self disciplined and I am reporting to a 'sponsor' who monitors my progress. I mention the power of an accountability buddy later in this book, my sponsor is my food accountability buddy.

If you're reading this and are too struggling with any form of addiction to food, alcohol, drugs, sex, porn, gambling, technology which is affecting your physical or mental health, there is support out there. I encourage you to explore your local 12 step recovery program and attend with an open mind and an open heart.

Step 3
Ways to Stay Accountable

"Accountability breeds response-ability"

- Stephen Covey

While you're more likely to do something and be motivated to do it if you want to do it, sometimes you just *have* to knuckle down, be disciplined and get the work done.

After all, overwhelm and procrastination are two types of FEAR. Procrastination is a person fearing an outcome and responding with the inability to start any action, or just messing around.

Nobody really wants to procrastinate. Nobody wants to feel so overwhelmed that they're stopped dead in their tracks. When these episodes of procrastination come it is a time to reflect and ask questions:

"Why"?

"Why does this action feel so difficult?"

"What is one small step I can do now to progress me forwards in my goal?"

This is the point where you really do need a healthy dose of accountability to push you along.

So how can you stay accountable?

Staying accountable means taking responsibility for yourself and your daily actions. There are many ways you can be self-accountable and there are many ways you can involve others.

Could you do any of the following to stay accountable:

Share Your Goals

There's nothing like putting your goals out there to bring them to life. Whether you share them with family and friends, colleagues, social media friends or mentors. Sharing what you want and then stating how you will do it will take that goal from a *"want to"* to a *"here's what I'm going to do"* action.

If you just keep your goal in your head, it is easy to drift off from the steps needed to achieve it. It's harder to drift off the path of achieving a goal if you've told those closest to you what you're aiming for and they're asking you questions about it all the time.

Blog About It

Got a blog? Great! Not got one? Why not set one up? They're simple to create on a platform like WordPress, Tumblr, Medium or Blogger and you can post updates from your phone. You can document your journey as you go along and build a tribe or following as you do.

Make a Video Diary

In the same way a blog is a written diary of your steps towards your goal, a video diary is the way to do it that doesn't require you to write. There are many vloggers out there on YouTube giving a peek and insight into their lives and how they are creating the life they want to live by achieving their goals.

Getting people to subscribe to your journey means they will be notified in their inbox when you post a new video, being able to watch your videos and see how you're progressing.

Join `Groups on Facebook or LinkedIn

Depending on your type of goal, there is a Facebook or LinkedIn group for so many different topics.

Want to run a marathon? Join a marathon runners group!

Want to lose 60lb? Join the multitude of fat loss, transformation challenge groups.

Want to improve your pipeline and increase sales by 40% in the next quarter? Again, there will be business groups to help you and offer advice, stay accountable, connect with others and gain valuable insight and information along the way.

Get An Accountability Buddy

For me, this is THE MOST POWERFUL point.

Accountability buddies can work *for you*, or *with you*. By that I mean you can hire someone and they keep you accountable with no responsibility on your part to reciprocate the service, or you can work with someone and have a mutual agreement where you encourage one another along equally.

There are many types of professionals who use accountability as the backbone of their work to help others achieve their goals such as fitness coaches, business mentors and mindset coaches. Then there's communities out there in Facebook groups or you can get a personal accountability buddy and help one another along.

I check in with my sponsor daily and feedback with my food diaries and how they have impacted on my mood. We work through the OA 12 step program together.

I train 1-2-1 with my fitness coach once a week, learning the correct technique for weight lifting and also reporting into him when I train outside of our sessions (with photographic proof!).

I meet with my business mentor every couple of months and take an overview of my business performance and plan strategy for the next quarter.

My mindset coach also leads my accountability group on Facebook. I get the chance to speak with her 1-2-1 a couple of times a month and discuss my personal blocks and what is stopping me from achieving greatness. In the group we set 3 weekly actions and report back every Sunday evening on what we have achieved in that week, with proof.

Finally, for the last 2 and a half years I have had a personal accountability buddy. I've mentioned him before in this book. Ben is an old friend of mine who shares values and goals and we are there for one another every day. Not only does he do things like call me to get me up, as he lives in a different time zone and is always up when I need to be, but we check in with one another and keep one another on track. We share our action plans for the week and report back with proof that we have completed our agreed actions.

The above accountability help seems like a lot doesn't it? But you see, with the exception of my business mentor, all those people help me win at areas of life that are not currently bringing me any income. Areas of life not directly linked to bringing in money are the ones that are the first to get forgotten about in the day-to-day busy madness of running my own business.

Day to day, I am a communications coach for a bank of clients. Copywriting, social media management, photography, videography and auditing client comms is the work that pays the bills.

Yet, for me there are other areas of life that I need to invest my time into. I am working on my health - particularly my work with OA and my fitness goals. I am establishing myself as a presenter and speaker, helping small businesses and entrepreneurs to grow their businesses on social media. I am singing in a new band which does bring in an income, but it's my creative outlet and so much fun!

You see, I am working on my goals on the side of being a busy business owner and parent. If I didn't have all the support above, I'd go back to playing small and just concentrating on the actions that bring in the money for the mortgage each month.

That's not enough for me. I want to grow. So I have invested in accountability partners to accelerate my journey to my various goals.

An accountability partner can come in the form of a gym buddy, a running partner, a mentor, a colleague who will show you the ropes, a friend or family member. You don't necessarily need to invest any money into staying accountable but the trick is to find someone who is as dedicated and invested in their goals as you.

I've realised I'm sounding like that smug journalist who had all her life together in the morning routine chapter. Please don't hate me! It's taken a long two years to get to this point, and I don't feel like I've got it all together yet, or that I ever will, but I do feel a hell of a lot better. If I can help just one person to think about doing things differently, motivating you to start your own self discipline strategy which leads to you being happier and achieving awesome things, then it was worth writing this book.

Put Your Money Where Your Mouth Is

A great way to stay accountable is to put money on the line. Try handing over some cash to a friend or family member, and you agree to get it back when you achieve different stages of your goal.

If your goal is fitness related, there are apps you can download where you put money into a pot, and earn it back with every gym visit (it is linked to your smart watch steps and activity and can be GPS tracked so knows where your gym is!). Pact and DietBet apps are two examples.

Put Your Money Where You Don't Want!

On the flip side of earning your money back as above, you could also pledge to donate to a cause that you HATE if you don't complete your actions on time. You'd hate that wouldn't you? Donating to something you despise! What a great motivator!

I did this myself last year. I am always late on the school run. My son's teachers had a bit of a word at the end of the school year as my son had been late for school 27 times. That's a lot! And it's not his fault, it is mine.

I decided this had to stop, for his sake. So I wrote on my notice board that I would donate £5 every time I was late to the Donkey Sanctuary charity. Why? I really don't like donkeys. A bad donkey ride childhood experience makes me shudder when I think of the creatures. So I said every time I was late, I'd donate it to the Donkey Sanctuary. I was quite amazed how much this conscious shift work and am pleased to report that the donkeys only got £10 in total from me in the Autumn term.

Sorry donkeys.

Enter a Competition

This doesn't necessarily have to mean a sporting competition. If your goal is to be a writer or world-class photographer, software programmer or chef, there are competitions for every single walk of life.

Entering a competition is a great way to have a final or short-term goal along the journey. Training to win and then the actual competitive nature of your competition means you'll be focused on the prize.

If your main goal isn't sporting related, it's still a great little task to enter something like a 5k/10k run, a Crossfit competition, that golfing tournament, or swimming gala to help with your mental and physical performance.

If you own your own business, or your industry has sector specific awards, why not enter? I do this as part of my day job with my clients and it is a very rewarding process to reflect back on all the positives and achievements of your work or business.

Curb the Electronic Addiction

It's no lie that the modern world is addicted to smart phones and technology. While we have valuable information and content at our fingertips each day, helping us learn at an unprecedented rate, we also suffer at the hands of technology.

If you've ever been super motivated to sit down and begin working on your goal, you've probably experienced the drain and drag of getting sucked into the social media wormhole.

You know what I mean, you've seen a notification pop up on Facebook and the next thing you know you're viewing a myriad of food pictures, photos of the girl who you sat next to in Chemistry's baby and your third cousin's recent holiday snaps.

It's just unnecessary and a distraction!

Shutting down electronics while you focus on your goal is such a valuable exercise. In my day-to-day work with clients the first thing I get any of them to do is to download the Facebook Newsfeed Eradicator Chrome plugin. This means you can access Facebook, see your pages, groups and notifications, but the newsfeed is blank, and instead replaced with an anti-procrastination phrase.

Right now, today's phrase on the Facebook news feed eradicator is:

"Procrastination is like a credit card: it's a lot of fun until you get the bill." ~ Christopher Parker

Once the news feed eradicator is installed, it's time to think about moving your phone out of reach. Place it on the other side of the room. If it rings, you will hear it and be able to respond.

Turn off your emails, turn off the notifications on any other desktop applications like WhatsApp or Messenger.

Focus your mind and your efforts on your task in hand and you will be amazed at what you can achieve in what seems like a much shorter time.

If you are worried and concerned about the amount of time you spend on social media, you can install apps on your devices which block you from visiting certain apps and sites for different amounts of time. BreakTime is one such app where you can allow yourself allotted times in the day to view social media apps or sites, once your work is done. Moment is another which tracks the time you spend on your devices. It may shock you!

Personally, I found that deleting the Facebook app from my phone was the best thing for me. I noticed I was on Facebook for around 3 hours a day. That's 21 hours a week. I was losing almost a day of my life each week looking at other people's lives.

I made the decision to try it for a week and see how I felt. With no app icon there on my phone to click onto, I coped. It was strange at first but I decided to do it another week. And another. I managed 14 weeks without actively accessing my personal profile (I still had to manage accounts for clients) and I really missed nothing.

I now access Facebook only once a day and briefly. Because I am not using it as much, I don't have as many notifications. I have also found that I enjoy real-life conversations more. "Did you see it on Facebook?" people will say about their latest holiday or endeavour. It's refreshing to be able to say no, and hear their actual account of things going on in their lives.

Set Up Clear Rewards

Another way to stay self-accountable is to set up mini rewards along the way to your goal. If you have broken down your main goal into actions and you know what you're working towards you can decide and define points along the way as mini goal markers.

What will you do at these? How will you celebrate? How will you reward yourself?

Regularly Audit Yourself

Auditing yourself and your progress on a regular basis is extremely powerful when it comes to being self-accountable.

In Step 8 we go through this in more detail but I personally like to review my progress every Sunday. I try and do more of an in-depth self audit on the 1st of every month on my goals and how I am progressing towards the big someday dreams.

I ask myself what went well the previous month and also what didn't go so well. What would I do differently and how can I improve on this month ahead? I will then usually plan some goals for the month in my journal.

We will talk about this in more depth later in the book.

Track Your Progress

Tracking your progress, much like self-auditing is powerful so you know where you are at any given time with your goal steps.

If your goal is business or finance related, you may have a spreadsheet of targets that you fill in and assess each week to notice where you are in your journey.

If your goal is fitness related you may track your sporting achievements; time, reps, personal best stats in a workout journal, or an app like JeFit. You may take progress pictures (highly recommended for anyone on a fat loss or muscle building journey) or you may track your food in an app like MyFitnessPal to stay on the right path to your goal.

Tracking allows you to assess where you are, at any stage of the goal journey. If you do this regularly you can notice areas that need more attention, being honest and realistic about the time you are setting aside for your goal. It can help you see extra steps you may need to implement, more help you may get to reach out for.

It can be a chore to track, but it definitely helps you to know what you've already achieved and what is next to make your goal a reality.

Journal

I love to track my daily actions and plan them in a journal. Some people do this by blocking time off in their electronic diaries, others just put pen to paper.

I'm a big fan of the Best Self Co, Self Journal. The two-page-a-day spread gets you to block half-hour time blocks out for all your actions, a space for daily gratitude logs, your main goal and 3 actions you will take each day and then a space to share your wins and what you learned that day.

It has been one of the most powerful tools in my goal setting armoury and I can't recommend it enough. Just planning out my day, knowing how long things take and being realistic with time and logistics has helped me to feel in control. It has enabled me to plan realistic deadlines, say no to people when I can clearly see I don't have the time and also realise how long or how little things actually take.

It is wonderful to look back on the Self Journal and see all the action steps I take daily and assess how they are getting me towards my goal.

Time Track

Much like you can plan out your time above, tracking your time when working on a project can be really insightful.

For example, when I started my writing career I would have a to-do list that was as long as my arm. I would be overwhelmed at the thought of creating four blog posts, a press release and starting an eBook. It would take me days to often get out of the overwhelm fog and make a start.

When I went freelance and started working with multiple clients, I installed an application called PayDirt. It is a time tracking app that not only allowed me to set timers for the different projects I was working on, but I taught it to know which client I was working for, depending on a set of keywords. As I was visiting websites or logging into client websites or Facebook pages of a client, PayDirt would pop up and know which one I was working for, allowing me to start the timer.

Coupled with the Facebook news feed eradicator and planning out my tasks for the day in my Self Journal, I started to see with a fresh pair of eyes just how long (or how little!) tasks took.

For example, I quickly grasped that I could research, write, upload images and publish a 500 word blog post within an hour.

When in flow and writing on a subject I was knowledgeable and passionate about, I could actually write 1000 words in 25 minutes.

This meant I could complete a 10,000 word eBook within a working day quite easily! It was a shock to realise how little time things took, and time tracking as I went meant I was less inclined to be distracted by social media, texts or emails. It became a little competition too - me against the timer!

Had I not started time tracking, I don't think I would ever have realised the extent of what I am capable of. It also allowed me to change the way I work for my clients and see which ones I was over-servicing and which clients needed more time and attention.

I also adopted time tracking at home to help me with self discipline and my household chores. I am rubbish at cleaning. I really hate it because I always wrongly believe it will take me much longer than it actually does.

One day I made a list and timed myself as I went. I now know that the bathroom takes 6 minutes to clean, including scrubbing the bath and shower. It takes 17 seconds to feed my dogs. It takes 2 minutes 30 seconds to change my bed covers. It takes 48 seconds to take the bin out.

I found once I knew this, I had no excuse and I stopped putting as many things off. I'm nowhere near as organised and tidy as I'd like around the home but this small activity has helped me see that I have no excuse for not taking an extra 7 seconds to fold a towel, or put my shoes away.

Seek Feedback

The last point on staying accountable is to seek feedback from others who have achieved your goal or those who are willing to help.

Sometimes you can put the work in and sweat blood and tears to reach a goal, but if you're doing something wrong, or the long way round, you could be hampering your efforts.

Don't be scared to seek help or feedback from those you admire or look up to. People who have achieved success, as long as they're not a douche, are generally happy to help others who are looking to better themselves and achieve great things.

Step 4

How to Avoid Goal Overwhelm
The Foolproof Action Plan

"Success is sequential, not simultaneous"

"Focus is a matter of deciding what things you're NOT going to do."

"If you chase two rabbits, you will not catch either one."

Gary Keller - The One Thing

Firstly, are you overwhelmed? Is this the reason you are reading this book? Are you finding yourself procrastinating even though you know you don't want to be? It sounds like overwhelm! So what are the signs of overwhelm, and what can you do to overcome it?

Signs Of Overwhelm

- You don't know where to begin, no matter how much you think
- You're not physically or mentally able to start your task in hand
- You procrastinate and do everything BUT the task you've set yourself
- You get headaches or back aches from too much stress
- You forget important things
- You don't find pleasure anymore in the things you used to love

This is a reminder of earlier chapters, but just incase you've flicked to this bit, or forgotten, here is your overcoming overwhelm plan:

1. Clearly define what it is you want

2. Be as precise and clear as possible

3. Choose just one goal

4. Assess where you are now. What are you already doing to achieve your goals?

5. Follow the next foolproof daily action plan and focus on ONE THING at a time

Gary Keller, founded Keller Williams - the largest real estate company in the world before writing his best selling book, The One Thing.

The One Thing is a leading book that teaches you how to have a foolproof daily action plan to ensure your goals are consistently moving forwards, and you're not paralysed by procrastination along the way.

It is an exceptionally simple concept - which is what makes it such a success and it has allowed Gary to transform his own life, the lives of his employees at Keller Williams and his global readership who have adopted his One Thing principles.

Straight out of college, Keller began working as a real estate agent and set himself a 'someday' goal of becoming VP of the real estate company he worked for.

He achieved this goal within 4.5 years and focused on it every single day. When he left his original company and founded Keller Williams, he took his own goal setting measures and ingrained them into the company he created, focusing on education of real estate agents and applying his goal principles.

The result is that Keller Williams is now the largest real estate company by head count, and Gary's own book has established him as the leader not only in his field, but for entrepreneurs as a whole.

So how did he do it? What is The One Thing? And how can you follow it too as your foolproof daily action plan towards your goal?

The main idea in the book is based around this one specific question:

"What is the one thing I can do such that by doing it, everything else will be easier or unnecessary?"

Read that again a few times.

You can actually use it and apply it in so many areas of life. If you do nothing else after reading this sentence, get a copy of The One Thing. It is a book you will read over and over again and always find inspiration when you pick it up. Or buy the audiobook – it is worth every penny!

The whole book is based around the above and the power of organising every area of your life around that one specific thing you can do NOW that will progress you to the top of your goal pyramid.

His process looks something like this:

SOMEDAY GOAL

This is the ultimate dream. The one thing you want to achieve someday.

∧

5 YEAR GOAL

This is the 5 year goal. What would you like to achieve in the next 5 years?

∧

1 YEAR GOAL

What would you like to have to show for your hard work after a year? How will it move towards your 5 year goal?

∧

1 MONTH GOAL

What will you achieve in the next month to move you towards your 1 year goal?

∧

1 WEEK GOAL

What ONE THING can you do this week to move you towards your goal?

∧

TODAY GOAL

What ONE THING can you do today to move you towards your goal?

∧

RIGHT NOW

What ONE THING can you do right now such that by doing it, everything else will be easier or unnecessary?

Keller's concept is to drill down to the nitty gritty of that one task and ensure it is moving you towards your goal.

Success is sequential. We speak of people as an overnight success which really isn't true. Nothing happens instantaneously, success takes hard work and dedication, applying yourself consistently and with focus.

You can speed up success by adopting this principle and know that if you break down your goals into manageable daily actions, you will progress forwards systematically and sequentially, and more likely to achieve your goals.

Keller also likens this to the power of the domino effect. Every great change starts like falling dominoes.

The following is an excerpt direct from The One Thing;

"When you think about success, shoot for the moon. The moon is reachable if you prioritise everything and put all of your energy into accomplishing the most important thing. Getting extraordinary results is all about creating a domino effect in your life.

Toppling dominoes is pretty straightforward. You line them up and tip over the first one. In the real world, though, it's a bit more complicated. The challenge is that life does not line everything up for us and say, "Here's where you should start." Highly successful people know this. So every day they line up their priorities anew, find the lead domino, and work away at it until it falls."

Why Does This Approach Work?

Because extraordinary success is sequential, not simultaneous. What starts out linear becomes geometric. You do the right thing and then you do the next right thing. Over time it adds up, and the geometric potential of success is unleashed. The domino effect applies to the big picture, like your work or your business, and it applies to the smallest moment in each day, when you're trying to decide what to do next. Success builds on success, and as this happens, over and over, you move toward the highest success possible.

- When you see someone who has a lot of knowledge, they learned it over time.
- When you see someone who has a lot of skills, they developed them over time.
- When you see someone who has done a lot, they accomplished it over time.
- When you see someone who has a lot of money, they earned it over time.
- The key is OVER TIME. Success is built sequentially. It's one thing at a time.

Just like with the geometric progression, when you line up your dominoes correctly, it's actually the smallest thing that does the most. So when you determine what your first domino is and knock it over, the impact of your action will create a higher level of success.

What Is Your One Thing?

So now it is time to figure out your own one thing, and your foolproof daily action plan for achieving your 'someday' goal.

Here is an example of two different someday goals, and working backwards the steps that could be takes to achieve those.

	Example 1	Example 2
Someday goal	I will be a world-class speaker in my field of expertise	I will sell 1000 community housing projects
5 year goal	I will write a best-selling book about my expertise	I will sell 100 housing community projects
1 year goal	I will mentor someone I admire and look up to who is already doing this	I will sell 200 homes
1 month goal	I will touch base with those I have contacted to get feedback	I will hire three new employees to help sell my 200 homes in a year
1 week goal	I will contact as many people as I can about being my mentor	I will write and publish the job vacancy post
Today goal	I will draw up a hit list of relevant people who could be my mentor	I will make contacts to relevant candidates on LinkedIn
Right now goal	I will research the right kind of mentors for me	I will define the skills needed by my dream team members

It is important to note that this will change daily. You will reassess daily and apply the One Thing principle to each of your actions.

While I did mention earlier about not being able to perform two activities at once, you can still apply this principle above for every area of your life. Just make sure you're not attempting it at exactly the same time.

Apply The Domino Effect In Your Life & Business

Take a look at an aspect of your business or life. What's the first domino you need to topple for extraordinary results? In other words, what is the most important thing that will bring the best results in this particular area of life or business and make other things easier or unnecessary?

Define this one thing and focus on that until it is done. Incremental improvements each day will bring amazing results over time.
Remember the question asked over and over;

"What is the one thing I can do such that by doing it, everything else will be easier or unnecessary?" and apply the someday principle working down to discover the action for each area of your life:

1. Finances
2. Spiritual life
3. Physical health
4. Personal life
5. Business or career goals
6. Relationships
7. Your current job

Exercise: Foolproof Action Plan
>>> *Journal* <<<

Take the above seven areas of your life and complete the someday to right now sequence for each area. At the end of this exercise, it is a chance to present before yourself a daily action plan for every area of your life.

Again, remember you can't work on everything at once and depending on the length of time your RIGHT NOW task will take, you may not be able to progress all 7 areas of your life in one day.

If you do have the time, and you are also adopting time blocking methods, you may find that you can do one small action each day in every area of your life that will move you forward. Particularly if you are following the Miracle Morning routine. You will find that you DO have more time to plan and implement your own daily actions.

Step 5

The Bullshit Buster
Removing Blocks for a Procrastination-Free Journey

Let's get serious and let's get honest.

This is YOUR life.

Not your partner's life, your parents, your siblings. This is YOUR own life and it doesn't have to play out like a fantasy movie in your head! There has never been a better time to shape your own life, carve your own path and make your own success.

Yet not everyone does. Not everyone has the guts, the determination and, of course, the self discipline to achieve their own success.

Why?

The long and short of it - we get in our own way and into our own heads. We create bullshit stories that we allow to define who we are and stop us from progressing forwards.

So what are the most common blocks and how can you overcome them?

1.   Stop Waiting For The Right Time

There will never be a right time and your perfectionism is killing your dreams.

It's perfectly fine to dream all these business plans in your head, thinking you will become a global superstar and dreaming of your own desert island and private jet. However, they're no good stuck in your head all day long. Nobody is going to buy an idea in your head.

It's perfectly fine to think "I'll just lose these first 7lbs before signing up to that running club." Do it NOW. There is no time like the present!

We humans sit in front of our computers for hours, days, months and years getting bogged down in unnecessary perfectionism before even launching a beta version of our idea or product and finding out if people will even like or buy it.

A couple of years ago, I went into business with two fitness professionals and we planned to create an online fitness coaching company. We were three people with different ideas, values and visions in their heads, all fighting to be heard and create the company.

The first thing we created was the 'perfect' system. We bashed out idea after idea in our heads and knew exactly how we wanted our system to function and operate.

We sought advice from software developers and almost vomited in shock at our the 5 figure price tag to even get this idea off the ground, before we'd secured ONE SINGLE CLIENT.

Yet we went with it. Even though it felt like a massive investment and a huge risk. Just before launch, I had a bereavement which became a lot to bear and I ended up walking away from the business.

I can now reflect back and realise that we went about things the wrong way. There was no basic platform that we could upscale along the way –

we dive bombed into perfection and as such the idea took well over a year longer and thousands more than it needed to.

The pressure of finances and the differing opinions, coupled with this insane obsession to make everything utterly perfect meant we all parted as directors.

The failure on my part in this business taught me some great lessons and mainly the one about being obsessed with perfection. It doesn't exist. Truly. Perfection just does not come into play and it should definitely never hold you back from starting to work on your goals.

I'm really pleased to report that despite the crazy investment, the other two carried on and have created a brilliant and successful platform that is helping people all over the world. I still work together within this business, as a third party consultant and it's great to see how the perfection has dropped and the business is thriving.

Getting on and being successful is about being empowered to speed up the process - not slow it down with impossible perfectionism. Fire it out then tweak. Seek feedback. Learn as you go.

The same with more personal goals. If you want to win that golf tournament, stop fretting about getting into the right club and the right coach, just get down to the driving range and hit a few balls.

If you want to run that marathon, don't starve yourself for a week in the hope of shifting a few pounds first. Or worse, don't set out running the full 26.2 miles before training. It takes time and it takes a few times getting things wrong.

When we strive for perfection it is actually a reflection of our own self worth issues. If your perfectionism is totally grinding every plan to a halt, it might be an idea to see a professional mindset coach and try and reframe those destructive self-worth issues and worry over judgement.

2. Stop Pissing Around On Social Media

I've said this one earlier and I'll say it again (mainly because I needed to hear it and have truly changed my perspective on this one). Facebook, Instagram, Twitter, Pinterest it's all just such a distraction!

Why do we do it? We can't help ourselves. We sit there with loved ones at dinner, not engaging in conversation and instead looking and escaping into our devices. WHY?

Why (me included) do we do this? What are we escaping from? Why are we not paying valuable attention and time to those who we love dearly?

It's actually pretty tragic when you think about it. What will the long-term effect be on our children and the next generation? Are we breeding a tribe of ignorant people, who would prefer to busy themselves in an online world than talk to a human being in front of them?

In addition to the worrying effect on our social skills, social media is a time and energy drain. I installed an app called Momentum on my phone which tracks how long you spend on your phone each day and then breaks it down into how long you spend on different apps or sites.

When I first installed this app, it was around the time I was suffering with overwhelm and procrastination. I'd just established my own business and felt lost, like I was about to drown. I knew I was spending far too much time on social media and so downloaded the app to tell me just how much time.

This one particular day, the app gave me the news that I had spent 6 hours on my phone looking at Facebook. In one 24 hour period! 6 hours. That is ONE QUARTER of my whole day!

When you translate that to my lifetime, if I were to live to 80 years old, that would equate to 20 YEARS of my life.

Is Facebook worth robbing me of 20 years? What could I achieve in two decades by putting down the phone?!

Surprise surprise, as soon as this horrible truth hit me, I curbed my social media use and although it isn't perfect (I work for many clients and curate their social media so sadly have to be on it) with the implementation of the news feed eradicator it has helped me to focus my time on my goals and getting to where I want to be.

After this conscious realisation, it was 6 months later when I became aware that even though I'd cut down, I was still spending 3 hours a day on social media. That's when I decided to delete the app (and therefore the temptation to get lost in it) from my phone.

Try it for a week and see how you feel!

3. Stop Wasting Your Life On Box Sets

Binge watching your favourite TV series is definitely one of life's greatest pleasures. It is also sadly one of life's biggest time drains.

My husband loves the TV show Big Brother. Yesterday it flashed on the screen that it was "Day 44 in the Big Brother house".

44 days. One hour of edited footage broadcast each night.

I shouted to him:

"How many episodes have you missed of this series."

"Only about 3"

Well. You do the math. That's 41 hours of his life that he has wasted in the last 41 days on watching a TV show which is watching other people be bored and locked up in a house like some strange psychological experiment.

What could he have achieved in 41 hours? He keeps moaning that his physique is not where he wants it to be. 41 hours of work in the gym would've produced some solid results by now.

He constantly complains that he is exhausted. Well, firstly Big Brother is broadcast late at night, so no surprise there! But if he was really exhausted, go to bed an extra hour earlier and get in 41 hours more sleep over the course of just over a month!

Think about how much time you spend watching TV. Whether terrestrial TV, Netflix series or recorded catch up programmes. Are they enhancing your life? If you are a person who watches Soap Operas, I'd ask you - what do they teach you?

Could you be doing something more realistic, meaningful and worthwhile with your time? Could you be even braver and do what I did, could you turn off the TV for a whole week and see how much extra time it gives you?

Go on. Do it. Unplug it.

4. Realise That It's YOUR FAULT

This one is often a bitter pill to swallow.

Not happy with your body shape?

Your fault.

Not happy with your bank balance?

Your fault.

Not happy with your job?

Your fault.

Everything you do in life is a choice. It is YOUR choice. You choose what you get out of this life, and I hope by now after reading all these action steps presented to you, that you could shape your life dramatically if you applied just a few of these principles.

5. Take Responsibility

Following on from the point above (I know it's harsh and I don't blame you for feeling triggered) but once you can accept that things are your fault and your choice, you can start to take responsibility and change them.

>>> *Journal* <<<

I like to advise my clients to do a 'life audit' at this point.

Take every area of your life:

- Finances
- Career/Business
- Love & Relationships
- Body
- Mindset
- Fun & Recreation
- Family
- Personal Growth

With every area, audit it.

- What do you do well?
- What works great?
- What do you actually dislike?
- What do you attract into your life?
- What could you do more of?
- What could you do less of?

Let's use an example of career/business. Let's say you work in an office and you hate it. You know you are worth more and can do more. You long to leave your job, or be promoted to another department but at the moment it is a pipe dream.

Answer the questions above about your situation as it is right now. What do you do well in your job, what works great, what do you dislike, what do you want to attract more of when it comes to work, into your life? etc.

Once you've answered those questions you might realise what you actually love about your job - the skills and tasks. You'll realise what are your strengths and weaknesses.

Next it's time to TAKE RESPONSIBILITY.

Looking at all the complaints in each area of your life above, know that they are all your choice, and you can also choose to change them.

Let's go back to the career example above. You hate your job. You've established that. You've also established your strengths and the tasks you enjoy.

So how can you take responsibility and reclaim your power here?

- Could you take some more courses to sharpen your skills?
- Could you be mentored by someone in a position you want - shadow them and gain valuable experience?
- If you really want to leave, how will you get yourself noticed? Come up with a job-hunting battle plan. Get your CV standing out from the rest, get in touch with your professional contacts, scour LinkedIn etc
- Could you see an opportunity within your company to move sideways or be promoted?
- Could you speak up and raise your concerns, demonstrating your case for why things should be done differently?

As you can see, just taking a minute to audit where you're at now, and then take responsibility to change can have dramatic consequences.

I have known many people in my field of work who have experienced a mini meltdown when it comes to areas of their life, only to accept responsibility and take action. The hardest part is accepting fault; whether with anyone else or yourself, but once you can take responsibility you can be liberated to write your own script and carve your own path with confidence.

6. Are Your Tribe Your Biggest Block?

Motivational speaker, entrepreneur and author, Jim Rohn, once said "You are the sum of the five people with whom you spend the most time".

So which five people do you spend the most time with? What do they teach you? How do they make you feel? What are their own personal values, work ethic, motivation and drive?

Did you know, if you have an obese friend, you're more likely to become obese yourself! The people around us are huge factors when it comes to our own success.

Is your partner supportive of you and your dreams? Do they get as excited as you and respect your time to work on your goals? Or do they play the victim and make it all about them when you choose to focus on yourself?

Trust your gut instinct. You are the only person who can write the movie script of your life. You hold the pen and that pen is powerful. If you hate your boss, you need to understand and accept that they're writing their own movie script for you to fit into. Refuse that. Set boundaries, know your internal gatekeeper and do whatever it costs to get you to focus on your own personal goals.

The reality is that you're probably going to lose some friends along the way when it comes to achieving your dreams. Some people will get jealous, some will be triggered and you'll make them feel inferior.

That is NOT YOUR PROBLEM.

That is their own shit and if it's causing a problem in your life, it's time to let them go.

With other people like your spouse or parents, you're not just going to cut them out of your life, but you can protect yourself by quietly working away at your goals instead of declaring war on anyone who doesn't see and share your excitement for your vision.

It's the reason I love the Miracle Morning book by Hal Elrod as previously mentioned. You fit your extra work into your mornings at a time when other people are asleep. They don't even need to know about it. You work away diligently, knocking down your dominoes and knowing where you're going.

One day they will wake up and be like "shit you got super successful!". Yes. But remember, it didn't happen overnight.

7. Get Professional Advice From Experts

When I say professional advice, I mean the advice on the tools and tricks to complete your chosen tasks. Obviously, doing market research and seeking the opinions of others on a product or service can be valuable.

Yet if you need to fix a car, you would ask for advice from a mechanic, not a hairdresser.

Some people out there think they have expertise on a range of subject matter. Do your homework and check. Make sure there is proof in their pudding otherwise their expert advice could possibly derail your progress.

Don't be scared to ask for proof from those you hire to get you to your goal quicker.

Step 6

Sprint vs Slow

Your energy is not infinite. You do not have banks and reserves of energy to power you through 20 hour days and unlimited time working on your goal.

You need to protect your energy and you need to look after yourself.

Those who choose to go down this self discipline path and achieve great things definitely make a sacrifice. We all know that goals and dreams take time. But sometimes you can be a busy fool and leave yourself no extra energy to truly focus on your ONE THING and get your actions completed.

In this step, I encourage you to tune into your mindset and your body and learn to read yourself, to understand when to sprint and when to slow down.

During the industrial revolution when factories relied on employees working in shifts to keep the production line going, it was the norm to work 10-16 hours a day. Men, women and children all put in the hours to complete the work and get paid.

A number of union guidelines, international government papers and books were published in the late 19th century encouraging a change to working hours, but it was Henry Ford who became the pioneer and the father of the 8 hour working day in the early 20th century.

He promised to let his workers work 8 hours a day, for five days a week while guaranteeing the equivalent of six days pay. Productivity increased and this small change resulted in huge profits and results for Ford.

However, this was 104 years ago. When the world was completely different.

Our working environments are experiencing a contemporary overhaul. Look a giant companies like Google, Facebook and Tesla and look into their working practices. They implement benefits, perks and create working environments for us as we live and work *today*. Ford implemented his 8 hour day and 5 day week because it was the right thing for the time. So what is the right thing for this modern time?

We do things so much faster and better with the advances in technology. Many forward thinking companies of today are adopting measures for the modern day workforce. Working from home, flexi time, meetings done via video link rather than international travel. We work smarter, not necessarily longer.

Yet, as I write this, I know that I can work longer and it will benefit me. I am trying to cram in as much work as possible before the Summer holidays. As a parent, my childcare options become limited over the Summer. It has meant that I have been working early every morning before my son wakes, and then again in the evening when he has gone to bed. My days are a mixture of child-friendly activities bookended by the work I need to complete in order to get paid.

What a luxury! Being self employed means I can do this. If I were working the equivalent of an 18 hour day in an office, I think I'd get fed up of it and feel drained. It isn't for everyone, but this is a perfect balance for me in that I spend quality time with my son whilst also working on my business. It causes a shift in mindset and feels like a privilege rather than a curse – I get the best of both worlds.

I'm also limited in time in the mornings and evenings so I find I naturally work quicker and smarter. I have to get tasks completed before my son wakes so I am constantly working to self-imposed deadlines.

This is also known as Parkinson's law. Parkinson's law is the adage that "work expands to fill the time available for its completion." Or alternatively phrased as "the amount of time which one has to perform a task is the amount of time it will take to complete the task." So in a nutshell, choosing to cram my work into shorter time frames actually works to the rules of Parkinson's law and I find I do get it all done around being a mum.

I also know I can't do this long-term. Maybe four or five days maximum before I crash. I'm into day 3 at the moment and have planned a chilled out afternoon, knowing I need to top up the energy reserves later.

I'm not writing this to suggest that you should in any way follow suit. I'm just pointing out that a 9-5pm role, 40 hours a week doesn't have to be the norm, nor does it have to get in the way of you achieving your goals outside of your job.

There's 168 hours in each week, and if you're working 40 of them and sleeping for 56 of them what are you doing for the other 72 hours in a week? And could you dedicate some of those hours to self disciplined actions that will in turn lead to great habits and feeling happier and in more control of your life?

When Are You In Flow?

Being able to sprint definitely involves being in flow. What is flow?

Also known as 'being in the zone', being in flow is a term coined in positive psychology when your mental state of operation is at its optimum level. It's when you're fully immersed in an activity where you're fully focused, feeling energised, experience full involvement and enjoyment in the activity. You're completely absorbed in your action and you're losing the sense of space and time.

Have you ever experienced being in flow? If so, what were the circumstances around it? How could you replicate that for the times you're looking to sprint and get stuff done?

I recently had the use of a recording studio for a couple of days while recording the audio book version of this book. This studio was sound proofed and had no windows. I spent 18 hours there in total, drafting and amending chapters along with recording sections of the book. I absolutely loved it. Every single minute of it. I arrived at 9am and left at 3am and honestly, it felt like I'd been there about 4 hours. The next day I was expecting to be tired, but weirdly I wasn't.

I think the absence of windows and clocks had tricked my mind completely. I had no concept of time, and was just focused on getting my work done, enjoying it in the process. I've since worked from studios with no windows and clocks and loved it, once again tricking my mind on the concept of time. I have realised that this is my sweet spot and perfect environment when I want to get my head down and achieve goals in a short space of time, in one sprint. This is the right environment for me to be in flow.

I also know that even when nobody else is home with me, working from home rarely helps me be in flow, unless it is early in the morning and quiet. So if I have to do focused work that requires a sprint, I try and take myself away from home.

I also make use of shared co-working spaces where you pay to use the facilities. I am a big believer in energy and vibes from others and I love going to these shared working spaces in the city centre, feeding off the energy of other busy working people using the space.

When Do You Need To Slow?

It's all very well focusing on the need for speed in life and work, but it's equally important to slow too.

If you were a regular gym goer, your trainer would always emphasise the importance of a rest day. You can't keep your foot on the gas and slowing down is equally as important as speeding up.

Planning in times to slow down can also act as a reward and drive you to achieve your goals in your sprint periods. If you know you have some down time planned in, use it to fuel you to get finished.

A friend of mine who owns his own business and tends to work away a lot makes sure he plans one evening a week for a digital detox. No phones, no TV, no computers, no tablets. It's the same rule for his whole family and they make sure they do something really worthwhile and spend quality time together with no distractions.

Sprint v slow is all about balance and you need to figure out the best way to make it work for you.

Dan Meredith who is the author of How To Be F*cking Awesome documents his own sprint and slow methods on his Coffee with Dan

Facebook groups and his process is fascinating.

He works in 90 day sprints and then 90 days slow.

In a 90 day period it's all work work work. He writes books in a matter of days, creates brand new online programmes overnight and launches new businesses.

Then, when 90 days are over, it's time to slow. Dan uses this time to still work on his businesses, but he tries to use this time to focus on fun and travel. Check out one of his many posts and videos of him playing on his jet ski, or taking himself off to a foreign city for the day. Honestly, the guy is ace and worth a follow if you don't already. Search 'Coffee with Dan' on Facebook.

Theming Your Days

Jack Dorsey, the CEO of Square and one of the founders of Twitter is the champ of sprinting. He worked 8 hours a day for both companies at the SAME TIME for a while when Square was being established. He said "The only way to do this is to be very disciplined and very productive." He didn't do it forever, 8 months I believe, but he was strict about having the weekends off completely and he also structured his working week by theming each day.

Jack Dorsey's days looked like this:

Monday:	Management meetings
Tuesday:	Product
Wednesday:	Marketing, comms and growth
Thursday:	Developers and partnerships
Friday:	Company structure and recruiting

Having this structure meant he always knew that if a task cropped up to do with marketing for example, he'd deal with it on a Wednesday. He was able to stay focused and work this way for an extended period.

If you're self employed and have flexibility with the way you structure your work, many entrepreneurs recommend the sprint method for the start of your working week.

So, if you can figure out your most important and time consuming tasks you do week in, week out, try and get those done at the start of the week, working late if you have to (this is what a few entrepreneurs I admire do). That leaves the rest of the week for creativity, growth ideas and actually working ON your business rather than stuck IN it. Or even better, it leaves you with the time to rest, relax, learn or be creative.

If you don't own your own business and your goal is around being more organised in the home, or better at work, or a health or fitness goal, could you adopt the same thinking? Could you challenge yourself to pick up the pace at the start of the week and complete those tasks leaving you with a bit of thinking and wiggle room for the latter end into the weekend?

Working Out Your Sprint v Slow Limits

So for you, do you know your own Sprint v Slow limits?

Do you know how much you can take on and the point at which you really need to slow it all down?

Do you know your weekly non-negotiable tasks in your life and business that MUST be completed? The tasks that you could maybe look to start completing at the start of the week, freeing up time later in the week for those slower days?

Have you been pushing too hard and over training? Are you giving your body the rest it needs? Are you eating enough ahead of that sporting competition, to give you the edge?

When was the last time you went on holiday and truly switched off? We are so connected to our devices these days that it has almost become the norm to still be in contact with the office when we are away, which never fully allows our brains and bodies the chance to rest and recover.

So, if you are feeling the burn of burn out and know that a slow down process is well overdue, could your ONE THING today be to do just that for yourself?

A massage, a 10 minute meditation, a chat over a cup of coffee with a good friend, a relaxing steam and sauna session at the gym, your favourite meal out for dinner? What could you do that will help you slow?

"I'm sick and tired of always being sick and tired!"

One thing that really stops me from being in 'flow' and being able to sprint is not actual tiredness, but perceived and false tiredness.

Try this exercise out for size today:

In the course of your day today, notice how many times people say "I'm tired" or a variation of it. "I'm shattered/knackered/f*cked/done in". I think you will be shocked! I believe that we say this out of habit, rather than actually listening to our bodies and assessing how we feel.

Another great exercise is this. For a week, try and STOP saying that you are tired. I did this and was really shocked how much I said it, and how it then made me feel… well tired!

Just like someone yawning in front of you will make your own mouth and throat twitch into the yawning action, saying you are tired makes you feel tired. I'd encourage you to ask yourself the question "Yes, but am I really?".

If you aren't actually tired, well then you've got more time and energy to dedicate towards your goals.

Step 7

How to Schedule Like a Boss

Many of the world's greatest entrepreneurs know that scheduling your daily tasks and being mindful of the time taken to complete them is the way to avoid overwhelm and procrastination.

The old cliché saying goes "time is money". If you happen to work on a fast paced production line, you know that every second is accounted for.

Much like the Sprint v Slow theory in the previous chapter, on a production line there is zero time for chatter and distraction.

You work to your absolute limit and best, diligently completing your own tasks and if you mess up, the whole production line stops. It is a huge responsibility but proof that focusing on your task in hand with zero distractions gets the job done!

So it's time to apply that principle to your own life.

Have you ever heard of a Pomodoro timer and the Pomodoro technique?

The Pomodoro Technique is a simple time management system developed by Francesco Cirillo in the late 1980s. Using a timer (remember the old style tomato timers you would have in the kitchen in the 80s?) well these timers are 25 minutes in length and break down your work into these increments, separated by 5 minute breaks.

These breaks or intervals are named pomodoros, the plural in English of the Italian word pomodoro (tomato), after the tomato-shaped kitchen timer that Cirillo used as a university student.

There are six steps in the technique:

1. Decide on the task to be done.
2. Set the pomodoro timer (traditionally to 25 minutes).
3. Work on the task until the timer rings.
4. After the timer rings put a checkmark on a piece of paper.
5. If you have fewer than four checkmarks, take a short break (3–5 minutes), then go to step 2.
6. After four pomodoros, take a longer break (15–30 minutes), reset your checkmark count to zero, then go to step 1.

Or if you are a person who works in a busy place with lots of distractions, or you need to speak with colleagues regularly to complete your work, you can choose to set the pomodoro to 25 minutes, and use the 5 minute break in between each one to touch base with your colleagues.

If you are interrupted during a pomodoro, you are encouraged to pause the timer and resume when you are distraction free.

There are apps that you can get on your phone and desktop which incorporate the pomodoro method, and allow you to track tasks completed and time taken. I have used this method myself for the last three years and found it particularly useful in my previous corporate role in a busy office.

If you do find yourself in a busy office getting distracted by colleague chatter then try wearing headphones. Even if you have no sound coming through them, you'll be shocked at how it helps people stop disturbing you.

The Self Journal

I have already mentioned this in Step 1, but I am a big fan of the Self Journal by Best Self Co for breaking down time blocks every morning and knowing what you will work on.

A simple paper diary and tracker, the Self Journal was borne after the developers interviewed the world's leading entrepreneurs to find out their secrets of success.

Scheduling tasks, gratitude, focusing on goals and sharing wins and lessons learned became the backbone of the Self Journal and I have to say, it has been one of the most powerful tools I have used since deciding to change my life and focus on my goals.

Other Time Blocking Apps:

Plan
www.getplan.co

Plan is simple and powerful and looks great with a clean user interface. It's part to-do list, part calendar, and all business plus loads of extra features that quickly set up blocks of time for priority tasks and projects.

Plan is very much like a shopping or to do list app but with a twist. The app shows your Google Calendar side-by-side with your to-do list, so you can drag-and-drop tasks into your calendar. (You decide whether or not others can see these focus blocks on your calendar.)

It also includes Day/Week/Month view options, as well as the ability to create lists and projects to further organise your tasks. Plan also gives you data including the average time spent on a task, or offers insights into key activities like taking lunch or exercising (by pulling keywords like 'walk' or 'lunch' from your calendar appointments).

Google Calendar/iCal

Whether you have an iPhone or Android, the in-built calendar is a brilliant option for time blocking. As with all time blocking planning, it is advised to decide on the time you will take on tasks first thing in the morning when planning your day and looking through your actions.

Your calendar can be broken down into 15 minute increments but you can colour code and add invitees, alerts and notes to your calendars to ensure that you are super efficient with your time blocking.

Don't forget to schedule in the stuff for you. Don't make it all about work work work. If your goal is to do with your body composition or a sporting achievement, make sure you put appointments with yourself in the diary. That way, you will be more likely to stick with your training, your meal prepping or your stretching for example.

PayDirt
www.PayDirtApp.com

On the flip side, if your job or goal in hand is more reactive than proactive and you're still looking for a method to see how much time a task has taken, I highly recommend PayDirt.

It isn't cheap as you pay a monthly fee to use it, but not only does it know what you're working on thanks to predetermined keywords, but it time tracks AND creates invoices which can be paid direct into PayDirt via PayPal or Stripe. Pretty cool eh?

Pitfalls with Time Blocking

When you first start to time block your tasks, you will be tempted to cram in too much and not be realistic about how long things take. This is completely normal.

When first beginning to time block, start small, with a couple of tasks. Decide on two tasks that you complete regularly and schedule a time in the morning and a time in the afternoon to complete these.

Follow all the other hints and tips in the book to avoid distraction so Facebook news feed eradicator, turn off emails, turn off your phone and deep dive into your tasks at hand.

Work ONLY and solely on that task. Once complete, notice how long it took you. Make a note of it and know that this task generally takes x minutes. This will come in handy in the future when you are time blocking.

It takes a couple of weeks to get used to assessing how much time you will need for all your tasks but once you are in the swing of it, you will wonder how you ever got so little done in the past!

Two Minute Tasks – JFDI

There will be many tasks you complete in your day to day life that don't really take much time at all.

If you have regular tasks in your life that take two minutes or less, the rule of thumb is JFDI which stands for 'Just f***ing do it!" or if you'd like a cleaner version how about "Do it, it's done!" (thanks to my friend Kerri for that one). It's also one of the easiest and greatest lessons in David Allen's

Getting Things Done book where he stresses the importance of tackling 2 minute tasks as soon as they crop up.

When I started time tracking, I also started time tracking chores and tasks in the home and was shocked at how little time some of them took.

When I then started using the Pomodoro technique, I found I used my 5 minute breaks to walk around and I might do a couple of these 2 minute tasks.

I kept a little note of how long things took. My two minute tasks are ridiculous, but I always put them off. Here's some of mine:

Make my bed – 30 seconds
Feed the dogs – 17 seconds
Take out the bin – 1 minute 30
Change the loo roll – 10 seconds
Put the dishes away – 2 minutes
Put a load of washing on – 1 minute 45 seconds
Put a load of washing in the tumble dryer – 50 seconds
Text my husband – 25 seconds

I remember looking at my list and laughing at the absurdity of it all. Why had I continued to think these small tasks were better saved for later?

Now I think JFDI in my head and I get them done. It still doesn't come easy and my natural default behaviour is to want to put it off, but when I JFDI it really does leave lots more room up in my head for other tasks and I do get a bit of a buzz ticking off these small tasks off the list.

Step 8

The Weekly Check in Process
Monitor Your Progress Every Step of the Way

So you've set a goal and you're going to achieve it! You're motivated and excited and you can't wait to get started.

Maintaining that momentum is the hardest part of achieving any goal. Monitoring and tracking your progress is the thing that will help you maintain that momentum.

The art of tracking your goals is a self discipline action in itself. If you don't monitor your progress you won't know if you're moving in the right direction and it's easy for those action steps to slip out of sight.

Tracking helps you focus.

In the last two years I have gained 40lb in weight. I can guarantee if I'd tracked my progress every week, asking myself honest questions about my behaviour around food and exercise I probably could have staged my own intervention. Alas, I didn't. My focus shifted onto my own business, I quit the gym and the weight crept on rapidly.

Now, this weight gain and noticeable change in appearance was actually a worthwhile experience for a couple of reasons. I developed a level of body confidence and acceptance through my weight gain, and it also taught me that I really am someone who goes off the rails with food and makes excuses about exercise if I'm not tracking or being made accountable.
I also noticed the negative effect my weight gain and lack of exercise had on my mental health. This was a chance to learn a lesson and realise it

wasn't just about numbers on the scale or the labels in my latest dress. So when I finally jumped back into tracking my nutrition and exercise, I immediately felt more mentally focused and clear – noticing correlations with my food choices and moving my body with having more energy and feeling better all round. Tracking also really helped me manage my compulsive overeating and emotional eating, bringing more awareness into my food choices.

The Sunday Self Audit

The Sunday Self Audit is inspired by Lewis Howes from The School of Greatness, who does admit that he doesn't get this right every week, but when he does it's valuable.

The idea is that you use time on a Sunday to look back at the week that has just passed and audit yourself. Then once you have a baseline of your week just gone, you can plan your week ahead.

It is something I've recently adopted into the mix and wow it's really thought provoking and a worthwhile exercise.

I don't know about you, but when I was employed in my full time job, every Sunday night I'd get 'the fear'. That flutter in your tummy anxiety for the week ahead where you'd think "Oh god what have I not done last week?" and "Oh crap, what have I got coming up this week?". Even though I run my own business, I still get this feeling! It's after a nice relaxing weekend with the family that the panic sets in.

That's why I love the Sunday night self-audit. It lays out everything on the table and helps me look at my upcoming week in a proactive, rather than reactive manner.

Every Sunday set aside some time, as much time as you can allow. 10 minutes will do but if you've got time for an hour, even better!

The point is to look back over the week and ask yourself some really important self-audit questions. Here are a few examples for your reference. You might choose to ask yourself the same questions every week, you might choose to answer a mixture, you might choose to just put pen to paper with no expectations and write down how you truly feel.

Example self-audit questions:

- What are my goals?
- What was my intention for last week?
- How many of my tasks did I complete?
- What was the best thing that happened / greatest win?
- What lessons did I learn?
- How much further am I towards my someday goal?
- What else could I do this week?
- Which areas of the week did I perform best?
- Which areas were a challenge?
- What is important now that wasn't before?

Once you've asked yourselves these questions, work out the plan for the week ahead.

- How much free time do I have this week?
- Where do I need to focus?
- What are my three main intentions for the week ahead?

Group Self-Audit

I've been part of mastermind groups where many people complete these kind of exercises and report back in every week. This was always the most beneficial way for me, because I knew I had a deadline and I knew I'd get kicked out of the very supportive group if I didn't do my Sunday assessment!

There are business groups out there where you can pay to join challenges and masterminds like this, or you could simply gather a small group of goal-getting friends and lead on this yourself. I use Facebook groups or WhatsApp for this to gather a group and check in with one another.

Keep checking on our Self Discipline Support Facebook group as there are plans to create our own Self Discipline mastermind groups in the future.

Different Ways of Tracking

Benjamin Franklin famously tracked his progress every day in 13 week cycles and asked his probing question each night; "What good have I done today?".

You don't necessarily need to track your progress daily, weekly works wonders too.

The Wheel of Life

One method you could use each week, which is visual and powerful is The Wheel of Life. If you've signed up for the workbook and 10 day email course, there is a copy of The Wheel of Life in the workbook for you to fill in.

The Wheel of Life can be drawn easily in any journal. Draw a circle and split it into 8 different sections and fill it in to give you a score out of 10 in each area:

- Finances
- Personal Growth
- Health
- Family
- Relationships
- Social Life
- Attitude
- Career

Ask yourself where you are right now in every area of your life. With 10 being the best and 0 being the worst.

I use the attitude wheel to describe my attitude to my goals and my general motivation to achieve them.

When you complete this exercise regularly, you start to notice patterns emerging and you can see which areas need more attention to bring up the score.

Tracking Spreadsheet

As described in the accountability chapter, using a tracking spreadsheet is another great way of seeing your progress written down each week.

It doesn't have to be anything complicated or fancy as it will be for yourself and possibly your accountability buddy or mentor to look over together and assess. You can use an online system like Google Sheets to be able to access it on the go, or share with an accountability buddy or mentor.

Keeping track is just the very best way to not let things slip. It doesn't need to take lots of time either, a simple tracking spreadsheet can be set up within an hour.

Tracking Apps

There are some great habit building apps out there where you can 'collect' each positive habit or action completed in order to get a streak of ticks or marks on your progress chart.

A few apps on the market at the moment that are great for this include:

Productive – Habit Tracker
Available on iOS for iPhone and iPad, Productive lets you set your own habits and actions in different categories and also set them in different day parts, days of the week, weekly or monthly. It will even send you reminders! For example, I have a reminder that goes off in a morning, afternoon and evening which reminds me to check my posture. If you complete the habit, you check the box and build up your habits gaining access to further levels.

Kick Butt – Goal Tracker
Kick Butt claims to have "iron fisted methods of motivation that go all the way!" You can forfeit payment for goals set, receive tough motivating messages across your devices and you can even link it to your social media accounts where it will post your failures and non-goal achievements out to all of your networks! Only for the committed.

Habitify
This is really clean and elegant in design and also includes a handy digital journal function. Habitify also produces graphs and data about your daily routines to help you see your week at a glance and where you might need

to reallocate more time and effort.

Hiring a Coach

Checking in with a professional coach in the area of expertise of your goal is something I highly recommend.

If that is a fitness coach, nutritionist, business coach. There are so many dedicated professionals out there who help people achieve their goals and ambitions.

You might check in with a fitness professional with weekly weigh-in, measurements and progress pictures.

You might check in with a nutritionist with a weekly food diary.

You might check in with a business coach every week reporting back on the actions you have taken to grow and market your business.

Step 9

Rest, Relax and Reward

"Take a rest. A field that has rested gives a beautiful crop."

- **Ovid**

We have already touched on the need for sleep and rewards along the way to achieving your goals, but in this chapter I want to dive into this a little more.

Firstly, when you start out on a path to success it can be difficult to gain the momentum needed to see your goals through to fruition. For example, if you're working towards a goal that is a year, five years or 'someday' away then it can be very easy to be derailed when a goal is so far out of reach and you have a lot of work to put in to get there.

Rewarding yourself along the way for achieving milestones helps break up the goal into manageable pieces. These smaller goals are really the necessary steps towards the large goals, and why shouldn't you reward yourself for your hard work, dedication and self discipline?

Rewards have been ingrained in corporate business through targets, bonuses and promotion structures. It is why business thrives, otherwise what is the motivation?

It's the reason why it is important to introduce rewards for your own 'business' whether that is actually the business you have set up and are striving to grow, or the business of you. By that I mean, your own body, health, mindset and personal goals.

Rest

You've worked all week. You've not just burned the candle at both ends – you've blow torched it and there is nothing left in the tank. It's time to rest!

It can't all be push push push as we learned in the Sprint vs Slow chapter. We can't always have the on switch on. We don't work like that.

It's really easy to ride the crest of a productivity wave and not factor in any rest.

So what steps could you take to make sure it is incorporated into your weekly routine?

Digital Detox

As mentioned, this is a great way to give the old brain cells a rest. A digital detox one night a month as an absolute minimum is super valuable, especially if you live with other people or you have a family.

Could you try and incorporate a device free evening once a week to focus on true human connection? No TV, no iPads, no mobile phones or laptops. Get this in one night a week as a minimum and I promise you, there will be absolute creative gems that come to you in this time when your mind is not pre-occupied and distracted by technology.

(If you do attempt this, please do come and tell us about it in the Facebook group! I really struggle to get my family to agree to this but when we do it makes us all feel so much better, connected and loved!)

Sleep

Not every person will be able to just chuck the towel in and schedule in a duvet day. We have commitments, careers and children to think of.
However, if you can't fit in a duvet day, you CAN fit in a few early nights to help you refresh and recharge.

I challenge you reading this to try and go to bed for one hour earlier every night for a week and notice how it makes you feel. Getting enough rest is associated with healthier body weight, greater motivation and smarter food choices. Sleep helps the brain to function much more efficiently, promotes learning, reduces stress, helps with problem solving and attention.

One way you can help yourself get to bed earlier each night is to set a bedtime alarm. Set it an hour before you want to go to sleep, have it go off and that be your signal to start your wind down.

Lack of Sleep and Heart Problems

Did you know? Every cell in the human body has an internal time mechanism according to Martin Young, Ph.D. in the University of Alabama at Birmingham Division of Cardiovascular Disease.

Martin Young has written many articles on the phenomenon of Daylight Savings and the clocks going forwards an hour. The loss of an hour's sleep leads to an increased risk of heart attacks for people with a history of heart disease. When the clocks go forwards one hour in March, there is a 10-24 per cent increase in the risk of having a heart attack the following Monday!

This is due to the circadian clock – the body's internal time rhythms which occur over a 24 hour period. The internal circadian clock is responsible for driving rhythms in biological processes, responding to changes in light and dark in an organism's environment. So when we disturb these natural rhythms with late nights, shorter mornings or something as simple as the clocks going forwards, our internal clocks don't have enough time to prepare our internal organs.

Scary stuff! So, it really is beneficial to get that extra hour of sleep in, if you can. If you can make it your routine – even better!

Reward

Equally as important when striving towards your goals is the need for rewards for completion, or rewards along the way.

If your goal is a body composition goal and the reason you're reading this book to instill self discipline when it comes to food and training, DON'T pick a food reward for hitting milestones.

Pigging out on pizza or doughnuts is not getting you closer to your 'someday' goal and the short term fix of sugar and comfort food is not beneficial to your long term goals. It messes with your head - trust me!

You might then be wondering how you can reward yourself along the way for milestones and mini goals that you achieve.

Here's our guide to ways to reward yourself for your tenacity, self discipline and goal-getting bad-assery!

1. Book a music concert for your favourite band
2. Learn a new skill and sign up for a class for something you have always wanted to learn
3. Have a proper duvet day off - stay in bed, binge watch your favourite Netflix TV shows, get in the snacks
4. Plan a mini holiday or short break with someone you love

5. Go for a night out with your friends - even better, go somewhere none of you have been and stay over. Make a weekend of it
6. Plan a night out at a comedy club (a great feel good night out!)
7. Book a table at your favourite restaurant
8. Organise a spa day
9. Book a massage
10. Book acupuncture
11. Get tickets to your favourite live sport; football, rugby, soccer, snooker, baseball, tennis, golf etc
12. Buy yourself something you've always wanted
13. Treat yourself to a new hair style, colour and cut
14. Throw a big party
15. See a movie in the middle of the day when the cinema is quiet
16. Go on a picnic
17. Buy an online short course AND complete it on a day off
18. Buy that expensive bottle of wine AND drink it!
19. Make your favourite meal with all the expensive ingredients
20. Take a break from your desk and buy yourself a candy treat
21. Call or spend the day with a family member or friend who inspires you
22. Get an adult colouring book
23. Create a private space at home for you to relax in
24. Dance and sing (this does wonders for the soul!)
25. Enjoy a long hot bubble bath
26. Crack open a bottle of Champagne
27. Go screen-less for an hour
28. Indulge in your favourite book
29. Host a board game night for you and your friends - no phones allowed!
30. Reorganise your home
31. Indulge in a shopping trip
32. Book the services of a personal shopper and buy clothes that suit your

shape

33. Organise a photoshoot
34. Volunteer at the local shelter
35. Write a letter to a friend or family member you haven't connected with for a while
36. Book a session with a personal trainer
37. Get a manicure or pedicure
38. Book a nutrition assessment by a professional and get some meal plans drawn up
39. Get a new tattoo or piercing
40. Test drive your dream car
41. Get fitted for new workout shoes at a specialist running store
42. Treat yourself to perfume or aftershave
43. Book a makeover at your favourite makeup counter
44. Get a spray tan
45. Get a cleaner
46. Sign up for a charity walk or run or endurance event like Tough Mudder
47. Sign up for a health subscription or cosmetic treat box
48. Take a guilt-free nap in the day!
49. Get your car valeted
50. Begin a 'rewards saving' challenge where you reward yourself with money for every time you reach a certain goal. I did this once with a gym challenge. Every time I went to the gym, I transferred £5 on my banking app to a savings account. By the end of my 16 week fitness goal, I'd accrued over £300 and bought myself a really nice outfit.

There are so many different ways you can reward yourself along the way. My personal favourite is the duvet day! I work so hard for such long periods, I love blocking out a day in my diary to do nothing. It works wonders for my creativity and energy levels and I truly feel like I've earned it when it happens.

Step 10

Failure v Success

"Our greatest glory is not in never failing, but in rising every time we fail."   **- Confucius**

Thomas Edison, inventor of the light bulb, tried over 1000 times to get a successful prototype of the light bulb. A reporter later asked him "How did it feel to fail 1000 times?" to which he famously replied "I didn't fail 1000 times. The light bulb was an invention with 1000 steps."

Unlike Mr Edison, so many of us are petrified of failure and never even get started on our wildest dreams and goals for the fear that we won't reach them.

But how will you know unless you try?!

We see it time and time again, so many people settle for mediocrity when there is no need to. If we could reach for our goals and not be held back by that which we're scared of, how exciting would that prospect be?

I recently experienced an incredible two-day seminar by UK neuroscience and behaviour specialist Dax Moy. Dax is responsible for the true transformation of his clients, both physically, emotionally and mentally thanks to his teachings of neuroscience which he blends with his fitness and nutrition training.

One thing absolutely stood out at that seminar and it was these two phrases:

"Tolerate nothing."

"Desire everything or require nothing."

You should not have to tolerate situations in your life that bring about misery, clip your wings or stop you from achieving your potential. Whatever area of life it may be.

It is difficult to see a life without someone or something whom you tolerate, but often it is the thing that is blocking you and it does need to go.

You should desire to have it all. You CAN have it all. Put in the work, be strategic, be focused. Quite simply, you work on it every single day. Without fail, and you'll get there! Even the smallest steps add up to huge achievements when repeated consistently over time.

That is the magic secret of self discipline right there ^ small daily actions, repeated consistently.

"Failure is not an option," NASA flight controller Jerry C. Bostick reportedly stated during the mission to bring the damaged Apollo 13 back to Earth, and that phrase has been etched into the collective memory ever since.

You Never Fail. You Always Learn

If you don't try, you won't know. You see, failure is life's greatest teacher. When you deem yourself to have 'failed' what can this perceived 'failure' actually teach you? What lessons can you learn?

Failure is one of the most powerful tools in reaching great success. Consider the greatest thinkers of our time; Einstein, Darwin, Freud, business mavericks and sporting legends all had the bravery to fly above the radar, go against the grain, make the waves, attract the attention and carve a path to success. Did they fail along the way? Of course!

Many modern-day employers embrace failure. Blue chip companies are known to seek out those who have experienced failure alongside success. For those employees who have been on both sides of the coin, they bring valuable and essential experience along to the party. They can demonstrate resilience, responsibility, perseverance and the wounds to show they have survived the business battle and lived to tell the tale.

"Possess as attitude of 'no fear' towards failure and you're on the path to success".

To be competitive, to meet targets, to stay ahead of the competition you have to stick your neck out on the line every single day. This is the same for your own non-business, more personal goals you're on the way to achieving. You have to push hard, you have to think big, you have to block out the fear of failure.

Perceived failure, while often painful at the time often results in our greatest growth and life lessons. We are able to retrospectively look back into our past and see the gifts in those things that went wrong.

It's a little superficial, but here goes. My 40lb weight gain over the last 18 months has been painful at times and I've very much deemed it as a failure at some points, but the gift in failing and piling on weight is that I have learned to love and accept my body. I realised I'd made drastic changes, and I had to work with what I had. I wasn't going to shed the weight overnight and instead of starving myself or embarking on a grueling exercise plan, I was supported through a period of self-love and learned to accept who I am RIGHT NOW. I have realised that I am the type of person that needs to take it one day and one action at a time when it comes to a weight loss goal and I've been able to see the patterns of past attempts and where I went wrong. As a result, I'm moving forwards again and focusing on how I feel, rather than the number on the scale and I feel free from the diet trap for the first time in my life.

Recently I worked for a client who had suffered a business collapse a few years ago. We spoke at length about his former business and he was still very much hurt from the pain of closing his business, laying people off and selling assets like his car. Even though he recalled this episode of his life with sadness, he said it was the best lesson he learned in business. His whole company ran on a specific piece of government policy that was never guaranteed to be around forever. The new government was elected, the policy abolished and the business lasted three months before it folded. Now he strives to have different sources of income within his business and never entirely rely on one revenue stream.

Another contact of mine was declared bankrupt in his early twenties. Just through being young, getting too much credit and then not having the means to live and pay off his loans, he didn't admit it to anyone until it was too late and bankruptcy was the only option. Now this might be perceived as a failure but you talk to him honestly about it and he will tell you it is the best thing that ever happened in his life. Two decades later and his attitude to money took on a new life after bankruptcy and he works to help others never experience this and save for the future.

Perceived Failures Exercise

The 10 day online course workbook takes you through an exercise where you reframe your perceived failures and get to see the gifts and positives that each brought to you. If you haven't yet signed up for the 10 day course and workbook, please visit www.mindandbodyworld.com/selfdiscipline

Conclusion

How is it possible to get two people, both trying to lose weight, at a restaurant perusing the menu and one orders the salad while the other says "I wish I had your willpower".

Willpower doesn't exist. It is a phenomenon that is fictitious. Self discipline is not something that you are born with, it is something that is *learned*.

You can learn it too. I promise.

Truth bomb alert!!!

I myself, I really struggle with self discipline.

It doesn't come naturally to me. I have to force it. I know I'm not the only one! Self discipline is something that many people do have to force out of their system. I know it takes me a considerable amount of effort to get out of the starting blocks, but once I do I'm away and sprinting to the goal getting finish.

I found the process of writing this book a real challenge and at the same time it was a joy to put together. I procrastinated a lot at the start and it took me a good couple of months to get my fingers onto the keyboard and get started. Yet once I'd made that start there was no stopping me!

Therefore, the fact you are even reading these words here on the page means I did just that – I created my plan and strategy of conscious disciplined actions, I was motivated to complete them and in time it became habit resulting in this book that you hold in your hands.

I have spent so much time and finances on learning how to have more self discipline in my life, to then ingrain positive habits and live a life that feels like I'm in control.

I've loved passing on what I have learned to my clients, friends and family. I've helped people to not *just* change, but truly transform and not *just* achieve their goals, but smash them out the water quicker, easier and with more enjoyment.

Focusing on self discipline for the book and teaching many of these points to others had a positive and knock on effect in many other areas of my life. My meals have been prepped, my gym sessions booked in and nailed, my dogs walked and meditation practiced daily. I'm on top of those mundane daily chores and life feels rigid at times, but it also gives me a huge sense of freedom, balance and relief that life is in working order.

That's the beauty of our methods for achieving self discipline in 10 steps. While you focus on your one thing, your big goal, you'll find you naturally gravitate to unconsciously improving other areas of your life.

After all, another of my favourite phrases always triggers me in good ways and bad:

"How you do *one* thing, is how you do *every*thing."

Delayed Gratification

In this fast paced, easy financed and aspirational digital world we live in, we don't really possess a lot of patience. When our grandparents were young, if they wanted something, an extravagant purchase for example, they would have to save and save until they could afford it. Our international culture of credit and having access to the internet and all the answers to all our questions means we have lost the art of patience.

In turn, we have lost the art of self discipline and delaying gratification for the greater good.

There is a very well documented test and study involving children and marshmallows, demonstrating how delayed gratification plays out to a young child. The essence of the study is a child is seated at a table and a single marshmallow is placed on a plate in front of them. The adult leading the study sits them down, shows the marshmallow and explains that they can choose to either eat the marshmallow now, or wait until they come back, not eat it, and they will get TWO marshmallows to eat.

If you Google this test, it has been repeated many times throughout many countries and is always fascinating and entertaining to watch these small 4 or 5 year old children practice self discipline and self restraint in order to wait it out and get the extra marshmallow.

Some kids just ate the marshmallow straight away. Other kids were quite ingenious and got around the rules and hardship of waiting it out by sniffing the marshmallows, licking them, nibbling one side and then trying to hide the bite marks. Some kids noticeably demonstrated restraint and self discipline by actively trying to distract themselves from the marshmallow by looking around, swinging their legs, shutting their eyes. For those children who showed self discipline and delayed gratification, they rewarded them with an additional marshmallow.

The most interesting thing from a 1972 marshmallow test by Stanford University and a professor named Walter Mischel wasn't the research and marshmallow tests conducted in the late 1960s, it was the years later that yielded the most surprising results.

Those children who waited it out, therefore delaying gratification to get their second marshmallow were all followed up and had higher exam results, lower levels of substance abuse, lower incidents of obesity, were better equipped to deal with stress and generally reported to have better social skills by their parents.

The children who dive in into the marshmallows straight away, on follow up years later did not perform as well as their self disciplined peers.

Right now, in this present moment, you might feel that you're not that great at delaying gratification. I know I wasn't. I'd be the kid scoffing the marshmallow within seconds! Yet the methods and strategies outlined in this book have been a life saver for me in my own quests to feel healthier, happier and more successful.

Research suggests that you CAN improve your self discipline and ability to delay gratification by adopting a few simple steps. So I hope you are able to take something away from this book and adopt even just a couple of steps to help you improve your own self discipline.

I look forward to everything falling into place for you, overcoming procrastination and achieving your own goals in these ten steps.

Remember, you make your own luck. Go get em!

Gemma Ray

PS – If you haven't already claimed your FREE 10 day online coaching course, please visit www.mindbodyworld.com/selfdiscipline.

To accompany this book, we have also created a dedicated Facebook group here: www.bit.do/selfdisciplinefacebook.

Connect with likeminded individuals who are also choosing to follow the steps outlined in this book. Get yourself an accountability partner, share stories and learning and celebrate each other's action steps and wins towards your goals.

For further reading, publications and additional resources, please visit www.mindandbodyworld.com

Printed in Great Britain
by Amazon